THIS IS YOUR **PASSBOOK**® FOR ...

TOW TRUCK OPERATOR

NATIONAL LEARNING CORPORATION®
passbooks.com

PASSBOOK® SERIES

THE *PASSBOOK® SERIES* has been created to prepare applicants and candidates for the ultimate academic battlefield – the examination room.

At some time in our lives, each and every one of us may be required to take an examination – for validation, matriculation, admission, qualification, registration, certification, or licensure.

Based on the assumption that every applicant or candidate has met the basic formal educational standards, has taken the required number of courses, and read the necessary texts, the *PASSBOOK® SERIES* furnishes the one special preparation which may assure passing with confidence, instead of failing with insecurity. Examination questions – together with answers – are furnished as the basic vehicle for study so that the mysteries of the examination and its compounding difficulties may be eliminated or diminished by a sure method.

This book is meant to help you pass your examination provided that you qualify and are serious in your objective.

The entire field is reviewed through the huge store of content information which is succinctly presented through a provocative and challenging approach – the question-and-answer method.

A climate of success is established by furnishing the correct answers at the end of each test.

You soon learn to recognize types of questions, forms of questions, and patterns of questioning. You may even begin to anticipate expected outcomes.

You perceive that many questions are repeated or adapted so that you can gain acute insights, which may enable you to score many sure points.

You learn how to confront new questions, or types of questions, and to attack them confidently and work out the correct answers.

You note objectives and emphases, and recognize pitfalls and dangers, so that you may make positive educational adjustments.

Moreover, you are kept fully informed in relation to new concepts, methods, practices, and directions in the field.

You discover that you arre actually taking the examination all the time: you are preparing for the examination by "taking" an examination, not by reading extraneous and/or supererogatory textbooks.

In short, this PASSBOOK®, used directedly, should be an important factor in helping you to pass your test.

TOW TRUCK OPERATOR

DUTIES

An incumbent to this position operates a tow truck and provides road service maintenance to disabled vehicles. Work consists of routine manual and simple mechanical operations of equipment. Direct supervision is received from a superior who may perform periodic inspection of work.

TYPICAL WORK ACTIVITIES

Tows all vehicles referred to the Division of Parking Enforcement operates a tow truck vehicle and car carrier (flatbed) to clear accident scenes; provides road service maintenance to disabled vehicles such as changing tires, replacing batteries and other minor mechanic service; tows disabled vehicles to garage when necessary work cannot be accomplished at the scene; performs minor maintenance work on tow trucks including maintaining oil, gas, grease, anti-freeze, tire inflation and cleanliness of truck; assists mechanics in repairing vehicles; performs related duties as required.

SUBJECT OF EXAMINATION

The written test will be of the multiple-choice type and may include questions on
1. Truck operation;
2. Geography and traffic laws;
3. Ability to understand and follow oral and written directions; and
4. Mechanical aptitude.

HOW TO TAKE A TEST

I. YOU MUST PASS AN EXAMINATION

A. WHAT EVERY CANDIDATE SHOULD KNOW

Examination applicants often ask us for help in preparing for the written test. What can I study in advance? What kinds of questions will be asked? How will the test be given? How will the papers be graded?

As an applicant for a civil service examination, you may be wondering about some of these things. Our purpose here is to suggest effective methods of advance study and to describe civil service examinations.

Your chances for success on this examination can be increased if you know how to prepare. Those "pre-examination jitters" can be reduced if you know what to expect. You can even experience an adventure in good citizenship if you know why civil service exams are given.

B. WHY ARE CIVIL SERVICE EXAMINATIONS GIVEN?

Civil service examinations are important to you in two ways. As a citizen, you want public jobs filled by employees who know how to do their work. As a job seeker, you want a fair chance to compete for that job on an equal footing with other candidates. The best-known means of accomplishing this two-fold goal is the competitive examination.

Exams are widely publicized throughout the nation. They may be administered for jobs in federal, state, city, municipal, town or village governments or agencies.

Any citizen may apply, with some limitations, such as the age or residence of applicants. Your experience and education may be reviewed to see whether you meet the requirements for the particular examination. When these requirements exist, they are reasonable and applied consistently to all applicants. Thus, a competitive examination may cause you some uneasiness now, but it is your privilege and safeguard.

C. HOW ARE CIVIL SERVICE EXAMS DEVELOPED?

Examinations are carefully written by trained technicians who are specialists in the field known as "psychological measurement," in consultation with recognized authorities in the field of work that the test will cover. These experts recommend the subject matter areas or skills to be tested; only those knowledges or skills important to your success on the job are included. The most reliable books and source materials available are used as references. Together, the experts and technicians judge the difficulty level of the questions.

Test technicians know how to phrase questions so that the problem is clearly stated. Their ethics do not permit "trick" or "catch" questions. Questions may have been tried out on sample groups, or subjected to statistical analysis, to determine their usefulness.

Written tests are often used in combination with performance tests, ratings of training and experience, and oral interviews. All of these measures combine to form the best-known means of finding the right person for the right job.

II. HOW TO PASS THE WRITTEN TEST

A. NATURE OF THE EXAMINATION

To prepare intelligently for civil service examinations, you should know how they differ from school examinations you have taken. In school you were assigned certain definite pages to read or subjects to cover. The examination questions were quite detailed and usually emphasized memory. Civil service exams, on the other hand, try to discover your present ability to perform the duties of a position, plus your potentiality to learn these duties. In other words, a civil service exam attempts to predict how successful you will be. Questions cover such a broad area that they cannot be as minute and detailed as school exam questions.

In the public service similar kinds of work, or positions, are grouped together in one "class." This process is known as *position-classification*. All the positions in a class are paid according to the salary range for that class. One class title covers all of these positions, and they are all tested by the same examination.

B. FOUR BASIC STEPS

1) Study the announcement

How, then, can you know what subjects to study? Our best answer is: "Learn as much as possible about the class of positions for which you've applied." The exam will test the knowledge, skills and abilities needed to do the work.

Your most valuable source of information about the position you want is the official exam announcement. This announcement lists the training and experience qualifications. Check these standards and apply only if you come reasonably close to meeting them.

The brief description of the position in the examination announcement offers some clues to the subjects which will be tested. Think about the job itself. Review the duties in your mind. Can you perform them, or are there some in which you are rusty? Fill in the blank spots in your preparation.

Many jurisdictions preview the written test in the exam announcement by including a section called "Knowledge and Abilities Required," "Scope of the Examination," or some similar heading. Here you will find out specifically what fields will be tested.

2) Review your own background

Once you learn in general what the position is all about, and what you need to know to do the work, ask yourself which subjects you already know fairly well and which need improvement. You may wonder whether to concentrate on improving your strong areas or on building some background in your fields of weakness. When the announcement has specified "some knowledge" or "considerable knowledge," or has used adjectives like "beginning principles of…" or "advanced … methods," you can get a clue as to the number and difficulty of questions to be asked in any given field. More questions, and hence broader coverage, would be included for those subjects which are more important in the work. Now weigh your strengths and weaknesses against the job requirements and prepare accordingly.

3) Determine the level of the position

Another way to tell how intensively you should prepare is to understand the level of the job for which you are applying. Is it the entering level? In other words, is this the position in which beginners in a field of work are hired? Or is it an intermediate or advanced level? Sometimes this is indicated by such words as "Junior" or "Senior" in the class title. Other jurisdictions use Roman numerals to designate the level – Clerk I, Clerk II, for example. The word "Supervisor" sometimes appears in the title. If the level is not indicated by the title, check the description of duties. Will you be working under very close supervision, or will you have responsibility for independent decisions in this work?

4) Choose appropriate study materials

Now that you know the subjects to be examined and the relative amount of each subject to be covered, you can choose suitable study materials. For beginning level jobs, or even advanced ones, if you have a pronounced weakness in some aspect of your training, read a modern, standard textbook in that field. Be sure it is up to date and has general coverage. Such books are normally available at your library, and the librarian will be glad to help you locate one. For entry-level positions, questions of appropriate difficulty are chosen – neither highly advanced questions, nor those too simple. Such questions require careful thought but not advanced training.

If the position for which you are applying is technical or advanced, you will read more advanced, specialized material. If you are already familiar with the basic principles of your field, elementary textbooks would waste your time. Concentrate on advanced textbooks and technical periodicals. Think through the concepts and review difficult problems in your field.

These are all general sources. You can get more ideas on your own initiative, following these leads. For example, training manuals and publications of the government agency which employs workers in your field can be useful, particularly for technical and professional positions. A letter or visit to the government department involved may result in more specific study suggestions, and certainly will provide you with a more definite idea of the exact nature of the position you are seeking.

III. KINDS OF TESTS

Tests are used for purposes other than measuring knowledge and ability to perform specified duties. For some positions, it is equally important to test ability to make adjustments to new situations or to profit from training. In others, basic mental abilities not dependent on information are essential. Questions which test these things may not appear as pertinent to the duties of the position as those which test for knowledge and information. Yet they are often highly important parts of a fair examination. For very general questions, it is almost impossible to help you direct your study efforts. What we can do is to point out some of the more common of these general abilities needed in public service positions and describe some typical questions.

1) General information

Broad, general information has been found useful for predicting job success in some kinds of work. This is tested in a variety of ways, from vocabulary lists to questions about current events. Basic background in some field of work, such as sociology or economics, may be sampled in a group of questions. Often these are principles which have become familiar to most persons through exposure rather than through formal training. It is difficult to advise you how to study for these questions; being alert to the world around you is our best suggestion.

2) Verbal ability

An example of an ability needed in many positions is verbal or language ability. Verbal ability is, in brief, the ability to use and understand words. Vocabulary and grammar tests are typical measures of this ability. Reading comprehension or paragraph interpretation questions are common in many kinds of civil service tests. You are given a paragraph of written material and asked to find its central meaning.

3) Numerical ability

Number skills can be tested by the familiar arithmetic problem, by checking paired lists of numbers to see which are alike and which are different, or by interpreting charts and graphs. In the latter test, a graph may be printed in the test booklet which you are asked to use as the basis for answering questions.

4) Observation

A popular test for law-enforcement positions is the observation test. A picture is shown to you for several minutes, then taken away. Questions about the picture test your ability to observe both details and larger elements.

5) Following directions

In many positions in the public service, the employee must be able to carry out written instructions dependably and accurately. You may be given a chart with several columns, each column listing a variety of information. The questions require you to carry out directions involving the information given in the chart.

6) Skills and aptitudes

Performance tests effectively measure some manual skills and aptitudes. When the skill is one in which you are trained, such as typing or shorthand, you can practice. These tests are often very much like those given in business school or high school courses. For many of the other skills and aptitudes, however, no short-time preparation can be made. Skills and abilities natural to you or that you have developed throughout your lifetime are being tested.

Many of the general questions just described provide all the data needed to answer the questions and ask you to use your reasoning ability to find the answers. Your best preparation for these tests, as well as for tests of facts and ideas, is to be at your physical and mental best. You, no doubt, have your own methods of getting into an exam-taking mood and keeping "in shape." The next section lists some ideas on this subject.

IV. KINDS OF QUESTIONS

Only rarely is the "essay" question, which you answer in narrative form, used in civil service tests. Civil service tests are usually of the short-answer type. Full instructions for answering these questions will be given to you at the examination. But in case this is your first experience with short-answer questions and separate answer sheets, here is what you need to know:

1) Multiple-choice Questions

Most popular of the short-answer questions is the "multiple choice" or "best answer" question. It can be used, for example, to test for factual knowledge, ability to solve problems or judgment in meeting situations found at work.

A multiple-choice question is normally one of three types—

- It can begin with an incomplete statement followed by several possible endings. You are to find the one ending which *best* completes the statement, although some of the others may not be entirely wrong.
- It can also be a complete statement in the form of a question which is answered by choosing one of the statements listed.
- It can be in the form of a problem – again you select the best answer.

Here is an example of a multiple-choice question with a discussion which should give you some clues as to the method for choosing the right answer:

When an employee has a complaint about his assignment, the action which will *best* help him overcome his difficulty is to
- A. discuss his difficulty with his coworkers
- B. take the problem to the head of the organization
- C. take the problem to the person who gave him the assignment
- D. say nothing to anyone about his complaint

In answering this question, you should study each of the choices to find which is best. Consider choice "A" – Certainly an employee may discuss his complaint with fellow employees, but no change or improvement can result, and the complaint remains unresolved. Choice "B" is a poor choice since the head of the organization probably does not know what assignment you have been given, and taking your problem to him is known as "going over the head" of the supervisor. The supervisor, or person who made the assignment, is the person who can clarify it or correct any injustice. Choice "C" is, therefore, correct. To say nothing, as in choice "D," is unwise. Supervisors have and interest in knowing the problems employees are facing, and the employee is seeking a solution to his problem.

2) True/False Questions

The "true/false" or "right/wrong" form of question is sometimes used. Here a complete statement is given. Your job is to decide whether the statement is right or wrong.

SAMPLE: A roaming cell-phone call to a nearby city costs less than a non-roaming call to a distant city.

This statement is wrong, or false, since roaming calls are more expensive.

This is not a complete list of all possible question forms, although most of the others are variations of these common types. You will always get complete directions for answering questions. Be sure you understand *how* to mark your answers – ask questions until you do.

V. RECORDING YOUR ANSWERS

Computer terminals are used more and more today for many different kinds of exams.

For an examination with very few applicants, you may be told to record your answers in the test booklet itself. Separate answer sheets are much more common. If this separate answer sheet is to be scored by machine – and this is often the case – it is highly important that you mark your answers correctly in order to get credit.

An electronic scoring machine is often used in civil service offices because of the speed with which papers can be scored. Machine-scored answer sheets must be marked with a pencil, which will be given to you. This pencil has a high graphite content which responds to the electronic scoring machine. As a matter of fact, stray dots may register as answers, so do not let your pencil rest on the answer sheet while you are pondering the correct answer. Also, if your pencil lead breaks or is otherwise defective, ask for another.

Since the answer sheet will be dropped in a slot in the scoring machine, be careful not to bend the corners or get the paper crumpled.

The answer sheet normally has five vertical columns of numbers, with 30 numbers to a column. These numbers correspond to the question numbers in your test booklet. After each number, going across the page are four or five pairs of dotted lines. These short dotted lines have small letters or numbers above them. The first two pairs may also have a "T" or "F" above the letters. This indicates that the first two pairs only are to be used if the questions are of the true-false type. If the questions are multiple choice, disregard the "T" and "F" and pay attention only to the small letters or numbers.

Answer your questions in the manner of the sample that follows:

32. The largest city in the United States is
     A. Washington, D.C.
     B. New York City
     C. Chicago
     D. Detroit
     E. San Francisco

1) Choose the answer you think is best. (New York City is the largest, so "B" is correct.)
2) Find the row of dotted lines numbered the same as the question you are answering. (Find row number 32)
3) Find the pair of dotted lines corresponding to the answer. (Find the pair of lines under the mark "B.")
4) Make a solid black mark between the dotted lines.

VI. BEFORE THE TEST

Common sense will help you find procedures to follow to get ready for an examination. Too many of us, however, overlook these sensible measures. Indeed, nervousness and fatigue have been found to be the most serious reasons why applicants fail to do their best on civil service tests. Here is a list of reminders:

- Begin your preparation early – Don't wait until the last minute to go scurrying around for books and materials or to find out what the position is all about.
- Prepare continuously – An hour a night for a week is better than an all-night cram session. This has been definitely established. What is more, a night a week for a month will return better dividends than crowding your study into a shorter period of time.
- Locate the place of the exam – You have been sent a notice telling you when and where to report for the examination. If the location is in a different town or otherwise unfamiliar to you, it would be well to inquire the best route and learn something about the building.
- Relax the night before the test – Allow your mind to rest. Do not study at all that night. Plan some mild recreation or diversion; then go to bed early and get a good night's sleep.
- Get up early enough to make a leisurely trip to the place for the test – This way unforeseen events, traffic snarls, unfamiliar buildings, etc. will not upset you.
- Dress comfortably – A written test is not a fashion show. You will be known by number and not by name, so wear something comfortable.
- Leave excess paraphernalia at home – Shopping bags and odd bundles will get in your way. You need bring only the items mentioned in the official notice you received; usually everything you need is provided. Do not bring reference books to the exam. They will only confuse those last minutes and be taken away from you when in the test room.
- Arrive somewhat ahead of time – If because of transportation schedules you must get there very early, bring a newspaper or magazine to take your mind off yourself while waiting.
- Locate the examination room – When you have found the proper room, you will be directed to the seat or part of the room where you will sit. Sometimes you are given a sheet of instructions to read while you are waiting. Do not fill out any forms until you are told to do so; just read them and be prepared.
- Relax and prepare to listen to the instructions
- If you have any physical problem that may keep you from doing your best, be sure to tell the test administrator. If you are sick or in poor health, you really cannot do your best on the exam. You can come back and take the test some other time.

VII. AT THE TEST

The day of the test is here and you have the test booklet in your hand. The temptation to get going is very strong. Caution! There is more to success than knowing the right answers. You must know how to identify your papers and understand variations in the type of short-answer question used in this particular examination. Follow these suggestions for maximum results from your efforts:

1) Cooperate with the monitor

The test administrator has a duty to create a situation in which you can be as much at ease as possible. He will give instructions, tell you when to begin, check to see that you are marking your answer sheet correctly, and so on. He is not there to guard you, although he will see that your competitors do not take unfair advantage. He wants to help you do your best.

2) Listen to all instructions

Don't jump the gun! Wait until you understand all directions. In most civil service tests you get more time than you need to answer the questions. So don't be in a hurry. Read each word of instructions until you clearly understand the meaning. Study the examples, listen to all announcements and follow directions. Ask questions if you do not understand what to do.

3) Identify your papers

Civil service exams are usually identified by number only. You will be assigned a number; you must not put your name on your test papers. Be sure to copy your number correctly. Since more than one exam may be given, copy your exact examination title.

4) Plan your time

Unless you are told that a test is a "speed" or "rate of work" test, speed itself is usually not important. Time enough to answer all the questions will be provided, but this does not mean that you have all day. An overall time limit has been set. Divide the total time (in minutes) by the number of questions to determine the approximate time you have for each question.

5) Do not linger over difficult questions

If you come across a difficult question, mark it with a paper clip (useful to have along) and come back to it when you have been through the booklet. One caution if you do this – be sure to skip a number on your answer sheet as well. Check often to be sure that you have not lost your place and that you are marking in the row numbered the same as the question you are answering.

6) Read the questions

Be sure you know what the question asks! Many capable people are unsuccessful because they failed to *read* the questions correctly.

7) Answer all questions

Unless you have been instructed that a penalty will be deducted for incorrect answers, it is better to guess than to omit a question.

8) Speed tests

It is often better NOT to guess on speed tests. It has been found that on timed tests people are tempted to spend the last few seconds before time is called in marking answers at random – without even reading them – in the hope of picking up a few extra points. To discourage this practice, the instructions may warn you that your score will be "corrected" for guessing. That is, a penalty will be applied. The incorrect answers will be deducted from the correct ones, or some other penalty formula will be used.

9) Review your answers

If you finish before time is called, go back to the questions you guessed or omitted to give them further thought. Review other answers if you have time.

10) Return your test materials

If you are ready to leave before others have finished or time is called, take ALL your materials to the monitor and leave quietly. Never take any test material with you. The monitor can discover whose papers are not complete, and taking a test booklet may be grounds for disqualification.

VIII. EXAMINATION TECHNIQUES

1) Read the general instructions carefully. These are usually printed on the first page of the exam booklet. As a rule, these instructions refer to the timing of the examination; the fact that you should not start work until the signal and must stop work at a signal, etc. If there are any *special* instructions, such as a choice of questions to be answered, make sure that you note this instruction carefully.

2) When you are ready to start work on the examination, that is as soon as the signal has been given, read the instructions to each question booklet, underline any key words or phrases, such as *least, best, outline, describe* and the like. In this way you will tend to answer as requested rather than discover on reviewing your paper that you *listed without describing*, that you selected the *worst* choice rather than the *best* choice, etc.

3) If the examination is of the objective or multiple-choice type – that is, each question will also give a series of possible answers: A, B, C or D, and you are called upon to select the best answer and write the letter next to that answer on your answer paper – it is advisable to start answering each question in turn. There may be anywhere from 50 to 100 such questions in the three or four hours allotted and you can see how much time would be taken if you read through all the questions before beginning to answer any. Furthermore, if you come across a question or group of questions which you know would be difficult to answer, it would undoubtedly affect your handling of all the other questions.

4) If the examination is of the essay type and contains but a few questions, it is a moot point as to whether you should read all the questions before starting to answer any one. Of course, if you are given a choice – say five out of seven and the like – then it is essential to read all the questions so you can eliminate the two that are most difficult. If, however, you are asked to answer all the questions, there may be danger in trying to answer the easiest one first because you may find that you will spend too much time on it. The best technique is to answer the first question, then proceed to the second, etc.

5) Time your answers. Before the exam begins, write down the time it started, then add the time allowed for the examination and write down the time it must be completed, then divide the time available somewhat as follows:

- If 3-1/2 hours are allowed, that would be 210 minutes. If you have 80 objective-type questions, that would be an average of 2-1/2 minutes per question. Allow yourself no more than 2 minutes per question, or a total of 160 minutes, which will permit about 50 minutes to review.
- If for the time allotment of 210 minutes there are 7 essay questions to answer, that would average about 30 minutes a question. Give yourself only 25 minutes per question so that you have about 35 minutes to review.

6) The most important instruction is to *read each question* and make sure you know what is wanted. The second most important instruction is to *time yourself properly* so that you answer every question. The third most important instruction is to *answer every question*. Guess if you have to but include something for each question. Remember that you will receive no credit for a blank and will probably receive some credit if you write something in answer to an essay question. If you guess a letter – say "B" for a multiple-choice question – you may have guessed right. If you leave a blank as an answer to a multiple-choice question, the examiners may respect your feelings but it will not add a point to your score. Some exams may penalize you for wrong answers, so in such cases *only*, you may not want to guess unless you have some basis for your answer.

7) Suggestions
   a. Objective-type questions
      1. Examine the question booklet for proper sequence of pages and questions
      2. Read all instructions carefully
      3. Skip any question which seems too difficult; return to it after all other questions have been answered
      4. Apportion your time properly; do not spend too much time on any single question or group of questions
      5. Note and underline key words – *all, most, fewest, least, best, worst, same, opposite,* etc.
      6. Pay particular attention to negatives
      7. Note unusual option, e.g., unduly long, short, complex, different or similar in content to the body of the question
      8. Observe the use of "hedging" words – *probably, may, most likely,* etc.
      9. Make sure that your answer is put next to the same number as the question
      10. Do not second-guess unless you have good reason to believe the second answer is definitely more correct
      11. Cross out original answer if you decide another answer is more accurate; do not erase until you are ready to hand your paper in
      12. Answer all questions; guess unless instructed otherwise
      13. Leave time for review

   b. Essay questions
      1. Read each question carefully
      2. Determine exactly what is wanted. Underline key words or phrases.
      3. Decide on outline or paragraph answer

4. Include many different points and elements unless asked to develop any one or two points or elements
5. Show impartiality by giving pros and cons unless directed to select one side only
6. Make and write down any assumptions you find necessary to answer the questions
7. Watch your English, grammar, punctuation and choice of words
8. Time your answers; don't crowd material

8) Answering the essay question

Most essay questions can be answered by framing the specific response around several key words or ideas. Here are a few such key words or ideas:

M's: manpower, materials, methods, money, management
P's: purpose, program, policy, plan, procedure, practice, problems, pitfalls, personnel, public relations

  a. Six basic steps in handling problems:
      1. Preliminary plan and background development
      2. Collect information, data and facts
      3. Analyze and interpret information, data and facts
      4. Analyze and develop solutions as well as make recommendations
      5. Prepare report and sell recommendations
      6. Install recommendations and follow up effectiveness

  b. Pitfalls to avoid
      1. *Taking things for granted* – A statement of the situation does not necessarily imply that each of the elements is necessarily true; for example, a complaint may be invalid and biased so that all that can be taken for granted is that a complaint has been registered
      2. *Considering only one side of a situation* – Wherever possible, indicate several alternatives and then point out the reasons you selected the best one
      3. *Failing to indicate follow up* – Whenever your answer indicates action on your part, make certain that you will take proper follow-up action to see how successful your recommendations, procedures or actions turn out to be
      4. *Taking too long in answering any single question* – Remember to time your answers properly

IX. AFTER THE TEST

Scoring procedures differ in detail among civil service jurisdictions although the general principles are the same. Whether the papers are hand-scored or graded by machine we have described, they are nearly always graded by number. That is, the person who marks the paper knows only the number – never the name – of the applicant. Not until all the papers have been graded will they be matched with names. If other tests, such as training and experience or oral interview ratings have been given, scores will be combined. Different parts of the examination usually have different weights. For example, the written test might count 60 percent of the final grade, and a rating of training and experience 40 percent. In many jurisdictions, veterans will have a certain number of points added to their grades.

After the final grade has been determined, the names are placed in grade order and an eligible list is established. There are various methods for resolving ties between those who get the same final grade – probably the most common is to place first the name of the person whose application was received first. Job offers are made from the eligible list in the order the names appear on it. You will be notified of your grade and your rank as soon as all these computations have been made. This will be done as rapidly as possible.

People who are found to meet the requirements in the announcement are called "eligibles." Their names are put on a list of eligible candidates. An eligible's chances of getting a job depend on how high he stands on this list and how fast agencies are filling jobs from the list.

When a job is to be filled from a list of eligibles, the agency asks for the names of people on the list of eligibles for that job. When the civil service commission receives this request, it sends to the agency the names of the three people highest on this list. Or, if the job to be filled has specialized requirements, the office sends the agency the names of the top three persons who meet these requirements from the general list.

The appointing officer makes a choice from among the three people whose names were sent to him. If the selected person accepts the appointment, the names of the others are put back on the list to be considered for future openings.

That is the rule in hiring from all kinds of eligible lists, whether they are for typist, carpenter, chemist, or something else. For every vacancy, the appointing officer has his choice of any one of the top three eligibles on the list. This explains why the person whose name is on top of the list sometimes does not get an appointment when some of the persons lower on the list do. If the appointing officer chooses the second or third eligible, the No. 1 eligible does not get a job at once, but stays on the list until he is appointed or the list is terminated.

X. HOW TO PASS THE INTERVIEW TEST

The examination for which you applied requires an oral interview test. You have already taken the written test and you are now being called for the interview test – the final part of the formal examination.

You may think that it is not possible to prepare for an interview test and that there are no procedures to follow during an interview. Our purpose is to point out some things you can do in advance that will help you and some good rules to follow and pitfalls to avoid while you are being interviewed.

What is an interview supposed to test?
The written examination is designed to test the technical knowledge and competence of the candidate; the oral is designed to evaluate intangible qualities, not readily measured otherwise, and to establish a list showing the relative fitness of each candidate – as measured against his competitors – for the position sought. Scoring is not on the basis of "right" and "wrong," but on a sliding scale of values ranging from "not passable" to "outstanding." As a matter of fact, it is possible to achieve a relatively low score without a single "incorrect" answer because of evident weakness in the qualities being measured.

Occasionally, an examination may consist entirely of an oral test – either an individual or a group oral. In such cases, information is sought concerning the technical knowledges and abilities of the candidate, since there has been no written examination for this purpose. More commonly, however, an oral test is used to supplement a written examination.

Who conducts interviews?

The composition of oral boards varies among different jurisdictions. In nearly all, a representative of the personnel department serves as chairman. One of the members of the board may be a representative of the department in which the candidate would work. In some cases, "outside experts" are used, and, frequently, a businessman or some other representative of the general public is asked to serve. Labor and management or other special groups may be represented. The aim is to secure the services of experts in the appropriate field.

However the board is composed, it is a good idea (and not at all improper or unethical) to ascertain in advance of the interview who the members are and what groups they represent. When you are introduced to them, you will have some idea of their backgrounds and interests, and at least you will not stutter and stammer over their names.

What should be done before the interview?

While knowledge about the board members is useful and takes some of the surprise element out of the interview, there is other preparation which is more substantive. It *is* possible to prepare for an oral interview – in several ways:

1) Keep a copy of your application and review it carefully before the interview

This may be the only document before the oral board, and the starting point of the interview. Know what education and experience you have listed there, and the sequence and dates of all of it. Sometimes the board will ask you to review the highlights of your experience for them; you should not have to hem and haw doing it.

2) Study the class specification and the examination announcement

Usually, the oral board has one or both of these to guide them. The qualities, characteristics or knowledges required by the position sought are stated in these documents. They offer valuable clues as to the nature of the oral interview. For example, if the job involves supervisory responsibilities, the announcement will usually indicate that knowledge of modern supervisory methods and the qualifications of the candidate as a supervisor will be tested. If so, you can expect such questions, frequently in the form of a hypothetical situation which you are expected to solve. NEVER go into an oral without knowledge of the duties and responsibilities of the job you seek.

3) Think through each qualification required

Try to visualize the kind of questions you would ask if you were a board member. How well could you answer them? Try especially to appraise your own knowledge and background in each area, *measured against the job sought*, and identify any areas in which you are weak. Be critical and realistic – do not flatter yourself.

4) Do some general reading in areas in which you feel you may be weak

For example, if the job involves supervision and your past experience has NOT, some general reading in supervisory methods and practices, particularly in the field of human relations, might be useful. Do NOT study agency procedures or detailed manuals. The oral board will be testing your understanding and capacity, not your memory.

5) Get a good night's sleep and watch your general health and mental attitude

You will want a clear head at the interview. Take care of a cold or any other minor ailment, and of course, no hangovers.

What should be done on the day of the interview?

Now comes the day of the interview itself. Give yourself plenty of time to get there. Plan to arrive somewhat ahead of the scheduled time, particularly if your appointment is in the fore part of the day. If a previous candidate fails to appear, the board might be ready for you a bit early. By early afternoon an oral board is almost invariably behind schedule if there are many candidates, and you may have to wait. Take along a book or magazine to read, or your application to review, but leave any extraneous material in the waiting room when you go in for your interview. In any event, relax and compose yourself.

The matter of dress is important. The board is forming impressions about you – from your experience, your manners, your attitude, and your appearance. Give your personal appearance careful attention. Dress your best, but not your flashiest. Choose conservative, appropriate clothing, and be sure it is immaculate. This is a business interview, and your appearance should indicate that you regard it as such. Besides, being well groomed and properly dressed will help boost your confidence.

Sooner or later, someone will call your name and escort you into the interview room. *This is it.* From here on you are on your own. It is too late for any more preparation. But remember, you asked for this opportunity to prove your fitness, and you are here because your request was granted.

What happens when you go in?

The usual sequence of events will be as follows: The clerk (who is often the board stenographer) will introduce you to the chairman of the oral board, who will introduce you to the other members of the board. Acknowledge the introductions before you sit down. Do not be surprised if you find a microphone facing you or a stenotypist sitting by. Oral interviews are usually recorded in the event of an appeal or other review.

Usually the chairman of the board will open the interview by reviewing the highlights of your education and work experience from your application – primarily for the benefit of the other members of the board, as well as to get the material into the record. Do not interrupt or comment unless there is an error or significant misinterpretation; if that is the case, do not hesitate. But do not quibble about insignificant matters. Also, he will usually ask you some question about your education, experience or your present job – partly to get you to start talking and to establish the interviewing "rapport." He may start the actual questioning, or turn it over to one of the other members. Frequently, each member undertakes the questioning on a particular area, one in which he is perhaps most competent, so you can expect each member to participate in the examination. Because time is limited, you may also expect some rather abrupt switches in the direction the questioning takes, so do not be upset by it. Normally, a board member will not pursue a single line of questioning unless he discovers a particular strength or weakness.

After each member has participated, the chairman will usually ask whether any member has any further questions, then will ask you if you have anything you wish to add. Unless you are expecting this question, it may floor you. Worse, it may start you off on an extended, extemporaneous speech. The board is not usually seeking more information. The question is principally to offer you a last opportunity to present further qualifications or to indicate that you have nothing to add. So, if you feel that a significant qualification or characteristic has been overlooked, it is proper to point it out in a sentence or so. Do not compliment the board on the thoroughness of their examination – they have been sketchy, and you know it. If you wish, merely say, "No thank you, I have nothing further to add." This is a point where you can "talk yourself out" of a good impression or fail to present an important bit of information. Remember, *you close the interview yourself.*

The chairman will then say, "That is all, Mr. _____, thank you." Do not be startled; the interview is over, and quicker than you think. Thank him, gather your belongings and take your leave. Save your sigh of relief for the other side of the door.

How to put your best foot forward

Throughout this entire process, you may feel that the board individually and collectively is trying to pierce your defenses, seek out your hidden weaknesses and embarrass and confuse you. Actually, this is not true. They are obliged to make an appraisal of your qualifications for the job you are seeking, and they want to see you in your best light. Remember, they must interview all candidates and a non-cooperative candidate may become a failure in spite of their best efforts to bring out his qualifications. Here are 15 suggestions that will help you:

1) Be natural – Keep your attitude confident, not cocky

If you are not confident that you can do the job, do not expect the board to be. Do not apologize for your weaknesses, try to bring out your strong points. The board is interested in a positive, not negative, presentation. Cockiness will antagonize any board member and make him wonder if you are covering up a weakness by a false show of strength.

2) Get comfortable, but don't lounge or sprawl

Sit erectly but not stiffly. A careless posture may lead the board to conclude that you are careless in other things, or at least that you are not impressed by the importance of the occasion. Either conclusion is natural, even if incorrect. Do not fuss with your clothing, a pencil or an ashtray. Your hands may occasionally be useful to emphasize a point; do not let them become a point of distraction.

3) Do not wisecrack or make small talk

This is a serious situation, and your attitude should show that you consider it as such. Further, the time of the board is limited – they do not want to waste it, and neither should you.

4) Do not exaggerate your experience or abilities

In the first place, from information in the application or other interviews and sources, the board may know more about you than you think. Secondly, you probably will not get away with it. An experienced board is rather adept at spotting such a situation, so do not take the chance.

5) If you know a board member, do not make a point of it, yet do not hide it

Certainly you are not fooling him, and probably not the other members of the board. Do not try to take advantage of your acquaintanceship – it will probably do you little good.

6) Do not dominate the interview

Let the board do that. They will give you the clues – do not assume that you have to do all the talking. Realize that the board has a number of questions to ask you, and do not try to take up all the interview time by showing off your extensive knowledge of the answer to the first one.

7) Be attentive

You only have 20 minutes or so, and you should keep your attention at its sharpest throughout. When a member is addressing a problem or question to you, give him your undivided attention. Address your reply principally to him, but do not exclude the other board members.

8) Do not interrupt

A board member may be stating a problem for you to analyze. He will ask you a question when the time comes. Let him state the problem, and wait for the question.

9) Make sure you understand the question

Do not try to answer until you are sure what the question is. If it is not clear, restate it in your own words or ask the board member to clarify it for you. However, do not haggle about minor elements.

10) Reply promptly but not hastily

A common entry on oral board rating sheets is "candidate responded readily," or "candidate hesitated in replies." Respond as promptly and quickly as you can, but do not jump to a hasty, ill-considered answer.

11) Do not be peremptory in your answers

A brief answer is proper – but do not fire your answer back. That is a losing game from your point of view. The board member can probably ask questions much faster than you can answer them.

12) Do not try to create the answer you think the board member wants

He is interested in what kind of mind you have and how it works – not in playing games. Furthermore, he can usually spot this practice and will actually grade you down on it.

13) Do not switch sides in your reply merely to agree with a board member

Frequently, a member will take a contrary position merely to draw you out and to see if you are willing and able to defend your point of view. Do not start a debate, yet do not surrender a good position. If a position is worth taking, it is worth defending.

14) Do not be afraid to admit an error in judgment if you are shown to be wrong

      The board knows that you are forced to reply without any opportunity for careful consideration. Your answer may be demonstrably wrong. If so, admit it and get on with the interview.

15) Do not dwell at length on your present job

      The opening question may relate to your present assignment. Answer the question but do not go into an extended discussion. You are being examined for a *new* job, not your present one. As a matter of fact, try to phrase ALL your answers in terms of the job for which you are being examined.

Basis of Rating

      Probably you will forget most of these "do's" and "don'ts" when you walk into the oral interview room. Even remembering them all will not ensure you a passing grade. Perhaps you did not have the qualifications in the first place. But remembering them will help you to put your best foot forward, without treading on the toes of the board members.

      Rumor and popular opinion to the contrary notwithstanding, an oral board wants you to make the best appearance possible. They know you are under pressure – but they also want to see how you respond to it as a guide to what your reaction would be under the pressures of the job you seek. They will be influenced by the degree of poise you display, the personal traits you show and the manner in which you respond.

ABOUT THIS BOOK

      This book contains tests divided into Examination Sections. Go through each test, answering every question in the margin. At the end of each test look at the answer key and check your answers. On the ones you got wrong, look at the right answer choice and learn. Do not fill in the answers first. Do not memorize the questions and answers, but understand the answer and principles involved. On your test, the questions will likely be different from the samples. Questions are changed and new ones added. If you understand these past questions you should have success with any changes that arise. Tests may consist of several types of questions. We have additional books on each subject should more study be advisable or necessary for you. Finally, the more you study, the better prepared you will be. This book is intended to be the last thing you study before you walk into the examination room. Prior study of relevant texts is also recommended. NLC publishes some of these in our Fundamental Series. Knowledge and good sense are important factors in passing your exam. Good luck also helps. So now study this Passbook, absorb the material contained within and take that knowledge into the examination. Then do your best to pass that exam.

———

EXAMINATION SECTION

EXAMINATION SECTION
TEST 1

DIRECTIONS: Each question or incomplete statement is followed by several suggested answers or completions. Select the one that BEST answers the question or completes the statement. *PRINT THE LETTER OF THE CORRECT ANSWER IN THE SPACE AT THE RIGHT.*

1. The BEST way to check for loose lugs is to   1._____

    A. twist them by hand
    B. use a lug wrench
    C. look for space between the nuts and the rim
    D. none of the above

2. Low tire pressure _____ chance of tire fire.   2._____

    A. improves handling and increases the
    B. makes handling more difficult, but lessens the
    C. makes handling more difficult and increases the
    D. none of the above

3. Leaking wheel bearing lubricant is MOST likely to result in   3._____

    A. a wheel lock up   B. a tire fire
    C. loss of traction   D. all of the above

4. In most vehicles, the brake low-air buzzer/alarm will come on when the air pressure is at   4._____
    _____ psi.

    A. 120   B. 60   C. 30   D. 40

5. To check steering wheel free play on vehicles with power steering, the engine   5._____

    A. must be on   B. must be off
    C. may be either on or off   D. none of the above

6. With the engine off and the foot brake applied for one minute, the air pressure should   6._____
    drop no more than _____ to _____ psi.

    A. 3; 4   B. 7; 8   C. 10; 12   D. 13; 15

7. With air brakes, it is wise to apply brake pressure _____ with hydraulic brakes.   7._____

    A. earlier than   B. later than
    C. at the same time as   D. none of the above

8. Auxiliary brakes or speed retarders are designed to   8._____

    A. protect the engine   B. stop the vehicle
    C. slow the vehicle   D. none of the above

9. On a long downhill grade,   9._____

    A. slowly apply and release the brakes
    B. use steady brake pressure
    C. fan the brakes
    D. none of the above

10. To make a right turn, start the turn from the _____ lane.   10._____

    A. middle of your   B. left
    C. left side of your   D. none of the above

11. When carrying a load, start braking _____ when empty.   11._____

    A. sooner than
    B. at the same time as
    C. at the same time, but apply more pressure than
    D. none of the above

12. To make a normal stop in a truck equipped with air brakes,   12._____

    A. ease off the brake pedal as the vehicle slows
    B. maintain steady pressure on the brake pedal until the vehicle stops
    C. apply light pressure and increase pressure slightly as the vehicle slows
    D. none of the above

13. To take a curve, slow down _____ the curve.   13._____

    A. before entering
    B. before reaching the sharpest part of
    C. on entering the sharpest part of
    D. none of the above

14. When turning, the BEST way to keep others from trying to pass on the inside is to   14._____

    A. flash the brake lights
    B. put the turn signal on early
    C. keep speed up
    D. all of the above

15. On snow-packed roads, reduce normal driving speed by   15._____

    A. 2/3   B. 1/2   C. 1/4   D. 3/4

16. When the road is wet, you should reduce speed by   16._____

    A. a little over 1/2   B. 1/2
    C. 1/4   D. 3/4

17. Ice will be MOST slippery when the temperature is _____ freezing.   17._____

    A. almost at   B. below
    C. well below   D. above

18. On wet pavement, worn tread on front tractor tires is MOST likely to result in   18._____

    A. hydroplaning   B. a blow out
    C. tire pressure loss   D. none of the above

19. Hard acceleration on a slippery surface _____ traction.   19._____

    A. improves   B. decreases
    C. does not affect   D. none of the above

20. The vehicle trucks MOST often run into is the one   20._____

    A. in front   B. to the left
    C. to the right   D. none of the above

21. Before backing, check behind by   21._____

    A. using all mirrors
    B. using mirrors and leaning out of the cab
    C. getting out of the cab
    D. using left-hand signal

22. At night, low-beam headlights let you see ahead about _____ feet.   22._____

    A. 450   B. 350   C. 250   D. 300

23. The image in a convex mirror will appear _____ it really is.   23._____

    A. closer than   B. farther away than
    C. the distance   D. none of the above

24. If you must slow down unexpectedly because the road ahead is blocked, warn drivers behind by   24._____

    A. turning on emergency flashers
    B. tapping the brake pedal
    C. motioning up and down with your hand
    D. stopping

25. After starting a lane change, you should   25._____

    A. move quickly into the new lane
    B. straddle the lane for a few seconds before continuing the lane change
    C. start the lane change and pause for a few seconds before entering the new lane
    D. none of the above

KEY (CORRECT ANSWERS)

1.	B		11.	A
2.	C		12.	A
3.	A		13.	A
4.	B		14.	B
5.	B		15.	B
6.	A		16.	C
7.	A		17.	A
8.	C		18.	A
9.	B		19.	B
10.	C		20.	C

21.	C
22.	C
23.	B
24.	B
25.	C

TEST 2

DIRECTIONS: Each question or incomplete statement is followed by several suggested answers or completions. Select the one that BEST answers the question or completes the statement. *PRINT THE LETTER OF THE CORRECT ANSWER IN THE SPACE AT THE RIGHT.*

1. When meeting an on-coming vehicle,

    A. move away from the other vehicle as far as possible
    B. move toward the other vehicle to encourage it to give you space
    C. keep your vehicle centered in lane
    D. stop your vehicle

1.____

2. To turn at an intersection where there are two turning lanes, use _____ lane.

    A. the outside or far   B. the inside or near
    C. either   D. none of the above

2.____

3. When backing a loaded truck, you need a helper because

    A. mirrors don't let you see the full length of the trailer
    B. mirrors don't let you see directly behind
    C. both mirrors must be used for a complete view
    D. someone needs to stop oncoming traffic

3.____

4. When driving in the city, look ahead as far as_____ block(s).

    A. one full   B. one-half
    C. one-fourth   D. two

4.____

5. To drive safely, look ahead _____ to _____ seconds.

    A. 12; 15   B. 8; 10   C. 4; 6   D. 16; 20

5.____

6. Use emergency flashers to warn following drivers

    A. it is safe to pass
    B. they are following too closely
    C. your vehicle is stopped
    D. there is a traffic accident ahead

6.____

7. In an emergency, to STOP quickly and CONTROL the truck, you should

    A. lock the wheels and keep them locked
    B. use the trailer brakes only
    C. lock the wheels, release, and lock again
    D. none of the above

7.____

8. Use of escape ramps USUALLY

    A. damages the vehicle's suspension system
    B. damages the vehicle's frame
    C. causes little or no damage to the vehicle
    D. damages the vehicle's tires

8.____

9. In a STRAIGHT truck, front-wheel skids are often caused by cargo placed too   9.____

    A. far forward   B. far back
    C. high in the cargo area   D. far apart

10. To put out a fire, aim the fire extinguisher at the   10.____

    A. flame   B. source of the fire
    C. area around the flame   D. none of the above

11. In handling an emergency ahead, which of the following statements is MOST often cor-   11.____
    rect?
    You

    A. can stop more quickly than you can turn
    B. can turn more quickly than you can stop
    C. cannot turn unless you first slow down
    D. cannot slow down unless you turn first

12. If the vehicle's air brakes fail, the FIRST thing to do is   12.____

    A. apply the emergency brake
    B. downshift
    C. pump the brakes to build pressure
    D. steer off the road

13. If you lock the rear wheels and begin to skid, the FIRST thing to do is   13.____

    A. accelerate quickly
    B. release the brake gradually
    C. release the brake immediately
    D. turn the vehicle into the skid

14. If you have to leave the road to avoid a collision, while off the road you should   14.____

    A. brake immediately   B. avoid braking until slowed
    C. accelerate slightly   D. get out of the cab

15. The BEST way to correct most trailer skids is to   15.____

    A. release the brake
    B. tap the trailer hand brake
    C. accelerate moderately
    D. apply the emergency brake

16. When requesting emergency assistance at an accident scene, the MOST important   16.____
    information to give is

    A. how the accident happened
    B. the location of the accident
    C. how many vehicles are involved
    D. your name

17. The BEST way to prevent fatigue is to schedule trips during   17._____

    A. daylight hours only
    B. hours you are normally awake
    C. weekdays only
    D. weekends only

18. Rust around lugs MOST often is a sign that the   18._____

    A. lug nuts are loose   B. rim is bent
    C. lug nuts are cracked   D. lug nuts are tight

19. *Thumping* a tire with a tire iron to check for proper air pressure   19._____

    A. is a quick and accurate method
    B. should only be done during enroute inspection
    C. is not an accurate method
    D. should be done daily

20. To check for air pressure loss in the brake system, watch the air pressure gauge while   20._____
you

    A. apply the foot brake with the engine off
    B. apply the foot brake with the engine running
    C. run the engine without braking
    D. downshift

21. Steering wheel free play should be no more than _____ degrees.   21._____

    A. 30   B. 20   C. 10   D. 15

22. As cargo is unloaded, remaining cargo should be moved to   22._____

    A. the rear of the vehicle
    B. maintain an even load distribution
    C. increase the center of gravity
    D. the front of the vehicle

23. The PROPER procedure for inspecting air tanks for oil contamination is to   23._____

    A. check for oil leaks or smears around air hose, line and valve connections
    B. open the tank petcocks and allow the tanks to drain
    C. apply service brakes sharply at 5 to 7 mph and note any mushy feeling or delayed
       stopping
    D. none of the above

24. The governed cut-out pressure for an air brake system should be between _____ to   24._____
_____ psi.

    A. 75; 100   B. 100; 125   C. 125; 150   D. 50; 75

25. As a vehicle's center of gravity is raised, the chance of rollover   25._____

    A. increases   B. decreases
    C. is not changed   D. none of the above

KEY (CORRECT ANSWERS)

1.	C		11.	B
2.	A		12.	B
3.	B		13.	C
4.	A		14.	B
5.	A		15.	A
6.	C		16.	B
7.	C		17.	B
8.	C		18.	A
9.	A		19.	C
10.	B		20.	A

21.	C
22.	B
23.	B
24.	B
25.	A

TEST 3

DIRECTIONS: Each question or incomplete statement is followed by several suggested answers or completions. Select the one that BEST answers the question or completes the statement. *PRINT THE LETTER OF THE CORRECT ANSWER IN THE SPACE AT THE RIGHT.*

1. In vehicles equipped with air brakes, braking begins   1.____

    A. as your foot presses the pedal
    B. a short time after your foot presses the pedal
    C. only after maximum foot pressure is applied
    D. only while using the emergency brake

2. On downgrades, speed retarders are used to   2.____

    A. stop the vehicle
    B. help slow the vehicle
    C. save engine wear
    D. maintain air pressure in the tires

3. On a downgrade, it is BEST to   3.____

    A. shift slowly   B. avoid shifting
    C. shift quickly   D. use the emergency brake

4. To take a curve to the left, the front of the vehicle should be steered   4.____

    A. close to the center line
    B. close to the outside shoulder
    C. near the middle of your lane
    D. none of the above

5. On slippery roads, applying the trailer hand brake before the foot brake   5.____

    A. is likely to cause a jackknife
    B. keeps the rig straight, preventing a jackknife
    C. may lock the trailer wheels, but will prevent a jackknife
    D. will cause a tire blowout

6. The PROPER time to downshift for a curve is   6.____

    A. on entering it
    B. just before its sharpest part
    C. before entering it
    D. in its sharpest part

7. Gripping the steering wheel with the thumbs inside the wheel   7.____

    A. is the proper procedure
    B. can cause injury
    C. can cause loss of control
    D. should be done only on slippery roads

8. Braking skids are GENERALLY

    A. more dangerous than acceleration skids
    B. as dangerous as acceleration skids
    C. less dangerous than acceleration skids
    D. none of the above

8.____

9. Flash the brake lights to tell following drivers that

    A. you are about to slow down for a tight turn
    B. they are following too closely
    C. you are about to change lanes
    D. your vehicle is stopped

9.____

10. With air-brake equipped vehicles, when the warning device indicates low air pressure,

    A. stop as quickly as possible
    B. pump the brakes to build up pressure
    C. accelerate to generate more air pressure
    D. decelerate to generate more air pressure

10.____

11. On ice-covered roads, you should reduce your speed

    A. by two-thirds
    B. a little more than one-third
    C. almost one-third
    D. by three-quarters

11.____

12. When the temperature is right at 32 degrees, freezing is MOST likely to occur first on

    A. curves   B. bridges
    C. hilltops   D. highways

12.____

13. The road is MOST slippery

    A. just after it starts to rain
    B. after it rains long enough to *wash* the road
    C. just as the rain stops
    D. at night

13.____

14. When a vehicle hydroplanes, you should

    A. release the accelerator
    B. gently apply the brakes
    C. stab the brakes
    D. use emergency flashers

14.____

15. To alert others of your location, it is BEST to

    A. use a slight tap on the horn
    B. use a loud blast on the horn
    C. avoid using the horn
    D. use hand signals

15.____

16. MOST air brake failures occur because of   16.____

    A. improper adjustment   B. loss of air pressure
    C. wear to the brakes   D. *riding* the brake

17. In backing, you see the MOST area to the rear in   17.____

    A. the right mirror
    B. the left mirror
    C. both mirrors about the same
    D. none of the above

18. If you have a tough time spotting oncoming vehicles because of poor visibility, turn on   18.____

    A. low-beam headlights
    B. high-beam headlights
    C. identification or clearance lights
    D. emergency flashers

19. When backing into an alley, you can see BEST if you turn to   19.____

    A. your left side
    B. your right side
    C. the side with the shorter distance
    D. the side with the longer distance

20. For a lane change, check the mirrors at least _____ time(s)   20.____

    A. three   B. two   C. one   D. four

21. At night, if forced to stop on or near the road, the SAFEST practice is to turn emergency   21.____
flashers on and

    A. put out reflective triangles and flares
    B. use identification and clearance lights
    C. leave your headlights and taillights on
    D. stand outside the cab

22. When approaching an oncoming vehicle on a narrow road, you should   22.____

    A. move to the left
    B. move to the right
    C. stay in the center of your lane
    D. none of the above

23. To make a left turn, start the turn   23.____

    A. as soon as you reach the intersection
    B. at the center of the intersection
    C. well before reaching the center of the intersection
    D. none of the above

24. To make a right turn in a straight truck, it is BEST to 24._____

    A. swing wide as you start the turn
    B. turn wide as you complete the turn
    C. start from the left side of the lane
    D. start from the right side of the lane

25. At highway speeds, look ahead as far as _____ mile. 25._____

    A. one-half   B. one-quarter
    C. one-eighth   D. three-quarters

KEY (CORRECT ANSWERS)

1.	B		11.	A
2.	B		12.	B
3.	B		13.	A
4.	B		14.	A
5.	A		15.	A
6.	C		16.	B
7.	B		17.	C
8.	A		18.	A
9.	A		19.	A
10.	A		20.	A

21.	A
22.	C
23.	B
24.	C
25.	A

EXAMINATION SECTION
TEST 1

DIRECTIONS: Each question or incomplete statement is followed by several suggested answers or completions. Select the one that BEST answers the question or completes the statement. *PRINT THE LETTER OF THE CORRECT ANSWER IN THE SPACE AT THE RIGHT.*

1. Which statement is MOST correct about vehicle length and following distance?   1.____

    A. Vehicles 40 to 60 feet long require the same following distance from the vehicle ahead.
    B. Longer vehicles require more following distance from the vehicle ahead than shorter vehicles.
    C. Following distance depends more on the type of vehicle ahead than the length of the truck.
    D. Following distance depends upon the speed of the vehicle.

2. A general rule for following distance is to stay one second from the vehicle ahead for each _____ feet of your vehicle's length.   2.____

    A. 20   B. 10   C. 5   D. 2

3. To put out a fire, continue until the   3.____

    A. flame is gone   B. smoke is cleared
    C. object is cool   D. firetruck arrives

4. If there is a fire in the cargo area, doors should be   4.____

    A. kept closed   B. opened quickly
    C. opened slowly   D. opened only slightly

5. Vehicle skids MOST often are caused by   5.____

    A. wet road   B. driving too fast
    C. worn tires   D. loss of air pressure

6. In recovering from a rear-wheel braking skid, MOST drivers err by failing to steer   6.____

    A. in the right direction   B. slowly enough
    C. quickly enough   D. none of the above

7. When coupling, the trailer should be positioned _____ than the tractor fifth wheel.   7.____

    A. slightly higher   B. slightly lower
    C. a great deal higher   D. a great deal lower

8. To support a trailer safely, lower the trailer landing gear with the crank until the   8.____

    A. gear touches the ground
    B. tractor stops rising
    C. tractor stops rising, and back off a turn
    D. gear touches the tractor

9. When turning a corner with a tractor-trailer, trailer rear wheels follow _____ the tractor rear wheels.

    A. a longer path than   B. a shorter path than
    C. the same path as   D. none of the above

9.____

10. To CORRECT a trailer drift when backing straight, turn the steering wheel

    A. away from the direction of the trailer drift
    B. in the same direction the trailer is drifting
    C. away from, then in, the direction the trailer is drifting
    D. in, then away from, the direction the trailer is drifting

10.____

11. To keep drivers from passing on the right when making a right turn with a tractor-trailer, position the

    A. tractor to block them
    B. trailer to block them
    C. tractor and trailer close to the curb line
    D. tractor and trailer away from the curb line

11.____

12. The BEST way to correct most trailer skids is to

    A. release the brake
    B. tap the trailer hand brake
    C. accelerate moderately
    D. turn into the skid

12.____

13. To check the fifth wheel coupling of a tractor-trailer, you must

    A. make a slow tight turn
    B. look under the rig
    C. move slowly backward
    D. make a fast left turn

13.____

14. A motor carrier who is also a driver (owner-operator)

    A. is not covered by the safety regulations which cover drivers
    B. must obey only those parts of the regulations which cover drivers
    C. must obey only those parts of the regulations which cover motor carriers
    D. must obey both the parts covering drivers and the parts covering motor carriers

14.____

15. With only a few exceptions, the Federal Motor Carrier Safety Regulations say a driver must be AT LEAST _____ years old.

    A. 18   B. 19   C. 20   D. 21

15.____

16. A driver cannot drive a motor vehicle for one year after a first-offense conviction for

    A. a felony involving a commercial motor vehicle operated by the driver
    B. driving a commercial vehicle under the influence of alcohol or narcotics
    C. leaving the scene of an accident which resulted in personal injury or death
    D. any of the above

16.____

17. Every driver applicant must fill out an application form giving a list of _____ during the previous three years.

    A. all vehicle accidents
    B. all motor vehicle violation convictions and bond forfeits (except for parking)
    C. names and addresses of all employers
    D. all of the above

17.____

18. At least once a year, a driver must fill out a form listing all motor vehicle violations (except parking) occurring during the previous 12 months.
The driver must fill out the form

    A. even if there were no violations
    B. only if convicted
    C. only if convicted or had forfeited bond or collateral
    D. only if the carrier requires it

18.____

19. If a driver applicant has a valid certificate showing successful completion of a driver's road test, the carrier

    A. must accept it
    B. may still require the applicant to take a road test
    C. cannot accept it
    D. may request a road test waiver from the Bureau of Motor Carrier Safety

19.____

20. A person with breathing problems which may affect safe driving cannot

    A. drive
    B. drive unless the vehicle has an emergency oxygen supply
    C. drive unless another driver is along
    D. drive except on short runs

20.____

21. Persons with arthritis, rheumatism, or any such condition which may affect safe driving cannot

    A. drive unless they are checked by a doctor before each trip
    B. drive
    C. drive on long runs
    D. drive without monthly medical examinations

21.____

22. Persons who have ever had epilepsy cannot

    A. drive unless another driver is along
    B. drive
    C. drive on long runs
    D. drive without monthly medical examinations

22.____

23. In order to be able to drive, a driver must NOT

    A. have any mental, nervous, or physical problem likely to affect safe driving
    B. use an amphetamine, narcotic, or any habit-forming drug
    C. have a current alcoholism problem
    D. have or use any of the above

23.____

24. If a driver gets an injury or illness serious enough to affect the ability to perform duties, the driver

    A. must report it at the next scheduled physical
    B. cannot drive again
    C. must take another physical and be recertified before driving again
    D. must wait at least 1 month after recovery before driving again

24.____

25. A driver may not drive faster than posted speed limits

    A. unless the driver is sick and must complete the run quickly
    B. at any time
    C. unless the driver is passing another vehicle
    D. unless the driver is late and must make a scheduled arrival

25.____

———

KEY (CORRECT ANSWERS)

1.	B		11.	B
2.	B		12.	A
3.	C		13.	B
4.	A		14.	D
5.	B		15.	D
6.	C		16.	D
7.	B		17.	D
8.	B		18.	A
9.	B		19.	B
10.	B		20.	A

21.	B
22.	B
23.	D
24.	C
25.	B

———

TEST 2

DIRECTIONS: Each question or incomplete statement is followed by several suggested answers or completions. Select the one that BEST answers the question or completes the statement. *PRINT THE LETTER OF THE CORRECT ANSWER IN THE SPACE AT THE RIGHT.*

1. When a driver's physical condition while on a trip requires the driver to stop driving, but stopping would not be safe, the driver   1.____

   A. must stop anyway
   B. may try to complete the trip, but as quickly as possible
   C. may continue to drive to the home terminal
   D. may continue to drive, but must stop at the nearest safe place

2. A driver may not drink or be under the influence of any alcoholic beverage (regardless of alcoholic content) within _____ hours before going on duty or driving.   2.____

   A. 4   B. 6   C. 8   D. 12

3. A driver must be satisfied that service and parking brakes, tires, lights and reflectors, mirrors, coupling and other devices are in good working order   3.____

   A. at the end of each trip
   B. before the vehicle may be driven
   C. only when the driver considers it necessary
   D. according to the schedules set by the carrier

4. The following must be in place and ready for use before a vehicle can be driven: 4.____

   A. at least one spare fuse or other overload protector of each type used on the vehicle
   B. a tool kit containing a specified list of hand tools
   C. at least one spare tire for every four wheels
   D. a set of spark plugs

5. If any part of the cargo or anything else blocks a driver's front or side views, arm or leg movements, or the driver's access to emergency equipment, the driver   5.____

   A. can drive the vehicle, but must report the problem at the end of the trip
   B. cannot drive the vehicle
   C. can drive the vehicle, but only at speeds under 40 miles per hour
   D. can drive the vehicle, but only on secondary roads

6. Any driver who needs glasses to meet the minimum visual requirements must   6.____

   A. drive only during daylight hours
   B. always wear glasses when driving
   C. always carry a spare pair of glasses
   D. not drive a motor vehicle

7. A driver may drive with a hearing aid if   7.____

    A.   the driver always has it turned on while driving
    B.   the driver always carries a spare power source for it
    C.   the driver can meet the hearing requirements when the hearing aid is turned on
    D.   all of the above requirements are met

8. A driver required to stop at a railroad crossing should bring the vehicle to a stop no closer   8.____
to the tracks than _____ feet.

    A. 5   B. 10   C. 15   D. 20

9. Shifting gears is not permitted when   9.____

    A.   traveling faster than 35 miles per hour
    B.   moving across any bridge
    C.   crossing railroad tracks
    D.   traveling down a hill steeper than 10 degrees

10. A driver of a motor vehicle, not required to stop at drawbridges without signals, must   10.____

    A.   drive at a rate of speed which will permit a stop before reaching the lip of the draw
    B.   sound the horn before crossing
    C.   proceed across without reducing speed
    D.   slow down only if directed by an attendant

11. When turning a vehicle, a driver should begin flashing the turn signals AT LEAST_____   11.____
feet before turning.

    A. 50   B. 60   C. 75   D. 100

12. Which of the following is TRUE?   12.____

    A.   If a seat belt is installed in the vehicle, a driver must have it fastened before begin-
ning to drive.
    B.   A driver may or may not use the seat belt, depending on the driver's judgment.
    C.   Seat belts are not necessary on heavier vehicles.
    D.   A driver must use the seat belt only if required by the carrier.

13. When a motor vehicle cannot be stopped off the traveled part of the highway, the driver   13.____

    A.   must keep driving
    B.   may stop, but shall get as far off the traveled part of the highway as possible
    C.   may stop, but shall make sure that the vehicle can be seen as far as possible to its
front and rear
    D.   may stop if the driver has to, but should do both B and C above

14. If a vehicle has a breakdown, the driver must place one emergency signal   14.____

    A.   100 feet in front of the vehicle in the center of the lane it occupies
    B.   100 feet in back of the vehicle in the center of the lane it occupies
    C.   10 feet in front or back on the traffic side
    D.   at all of the above locations

15. If a vehicle has a breakdown on a poorly lit street or highway, the driver shall place on the traffic side a   15.____

    A. reflective triangle   B. lighted red electric lantern
    C. red reflector   D. any one of the above

16. No emergency signals are required for a vehicle with a breakdown if the street or high-way lighting is bright enough so it can be seen at a distance of _____ feet.   16.____

    A. 100   B. 200   C. 500   D. 750

17. If a vehicle has a breakdown and stops on a poorly lit DIVIDED or ONE-WAY HIGHWAY, the driver must place one emergency signal   17.____

    A. 200 feet in back of the vehicle in the center of the lane it occupies
    B. 100 feet in back of the vehicle on the traffic side of the vehicle
    C. 10 feet in back of the vehicle on the traffic side of the vehicle
    D. at all of the above locations

18. Lighted flame-producing emergency signals, including fuses, may not be used with   18.____

    A. vehicles carrying Class A or B explosives
    B. tank vehicles, loaded or empty, which are used to carry flammable liquids or gas
    C. any vehicle using compressed gas as a fuel
    D. any of the above

19. A driver is required to turn on vehicle lights from   19.____

    A. one-half hour before sunset to one-half hour before sunrise
    B. one-half hour before sunset to sunrise
    C. one-half hour after sunset to one-half hour before sunrise
    D. sunset to one-half hour before sunrise

20. When lights are required on the highway, a driver shall use the high beam EXCEPT when within _____ feet of an oncoming vehicle or a vehicle the driver is following.   20.____

    A. 500   B. 400   C. 200   D. 100

21. When lights are required, a driver may use lower beam lights when   21.____

    A. fog, dust, or other such conditions exist
    B. approaching tunnels or bridges
    C. driving on one-way highways
    D. within 1000 feet of business areas or where people live

22. Every driver involved in an accident must follow the safety regulation procedures when-ever an injury or death is involved or if   22.____

    A. the accident is caused by the driver and property damage of over $2000 results
    B. property damage of over $2000 results, no matter who is at fault
    C. property damage of over $100 results
    D. property damage of any kind results

23. If a driver strikes a parked vehicle, the driver should FIRST stop and   23._____

    A. call the local police
    B. call the carrier
    C. try to find the driver or owner of the parked vehicle
    D. estimate the damages

24. When a driver receives notice of license or permit revocation, suspension or other with-   24._____
    drawal action, the driver must

    A. notify the carrier within 72 hours
    B. notify the carrier within one week
    C. notify the carrier before the end of the next business day
    D. take no action since the carrier will get a notice

25. Except in emergencies, no driver shall allow a vehicle to be driven by any other person   25._____

    A. except by those the driver knows are capable
    B. except on roads with little or no traffic
    C. except by those allowed by the carrier to do it
    D. unless the driver goes along with the person driving

_____

KEY (CORRECT ANSWERS)

1.	D		11.	D
2.	A		12.	A
3.	B		13.	D
4.	A		14.	D
5.	B		15.	D
6.	B		16.	C
7.	D		17.	D
8.	C		18.	D
9.	C		19.	C
10.	A		20.	A

21.	A
22.	D
23.	C
24.	C
25.	C

_____

TEST 3

DIRECTIONS: Each question or incomplete statement is followed by several suggested answers or completions. Select the one that BEST answers the question or completes the statement. *PRINT THE LETTER OF THE CORRECT ANSWER IN THE SPACE AT THE RIGHT.*

1. A person may ride inside a vehicle's closed body or trailer ONLY

    A. on short runs
    B. if there is an easy way to get out from the inside
    C. if the inside of the body or trailer is lighted
    D. if there is no cargo in it

1.____

2. If carbon monoxide is inside a vehicle or if a mechanical problem may produce a carbon monoxide danger, the vehicle may

    A. be sent out and driven so long as the windows are left open
    B. not be sent out or driven
    C. be sent out and driven only if the carrier decides the vehicle has to be used
    D. be sent out and driven on short runs

2.____

3. No motor vehicle shall be operated out of gear EXCEPT

    A. when fuel must be saved
    B. on hills which are less than 20 degrees
    C. when it is necessary for stopping or shifting gears
    D. when the vehicle's speed is under 25 miles per hour

3.____

4. Under the Federal Motor Carrier Safety Regulations, no vehicle may be driven

    A. until a list of all missing or defective equipment has been prepared and given to the carrier
    B. until all equipment has been inspected and replacements for defective parts have been ordered
    C. unless all missing equipment is to be replaced no later than the end of the vehicle's next run
    D. until it meets all of the equipment requirements of the regulations

4.____

5. Minimum requirements for lighting, reflecting and electrical equipment and devices on buses and trucks are

    A. set by the vehicle makers
    B. set by the National Safety Council
    C. specified in the safety regulations
    D. set by the trucking associations

5.____

6. Every motor vehicle which has a load sticking out over its sides must be specifically marked with flags and lamps.
Additional flags and lamps must be added if the load or tailgate sticks out beyond the rear of the vehicle by more than _____ feet.

    A. 2   B. 4   C. 6   D. 8

6.____

7. Every vehicle shall have a parking brake system which will hold it, no matter what its load, on   7.____

    A. any grade on which it is operated which is free from ice and snow
    B. all grades under 15 degrees which are free from ice and snow
    C. all grades under 20 degrees which are free from ice and snow
    D. all grades under 25 degrees which are free from ice and snow

8. A portable heater may NOT be used in any vehicle cab   8.____

    A. unless the heater is secured
    B. unless the heater is of the electric filament type
    C. at any time
    D. without approval from the carrier

9. A driver is not generally allowed to drive for more than _____ hours following 8 straight hours off duty.   9.____

    A. 6   B. 8   C. 10   D. 12

10. Most drivers of large vehicles are NOT allowed to drive after they have been *on duty* for _____ hours.   10.____

    A. 16   B. 15   C. 14   D. 12

11. Generally, a driver may not be *on duty* for more than _____ hours in any 7 straight days.   11.____

    A. 40   B. 50   C. 60   D. 70

12. When a driver is riding in a vehicle, but is not driving and has no other responsibility, such time shall be counted as on-duty   12.____

    A. time
    B. time unless the driver is allowed 8 straight hours off duty upon arrival at the destination
    C. time unless the driver is allowed 6 straight hours off duty upon arrival at the destination
    D. time unless the driver is allowed 4 straight hours off duty upon arrival at the destination

13. Every driver must prepare an original and one copy of the driver's record of duty status which must be kept current by updating it   13.____

    A. every time a change of duty status is made
    B. every 24 hours
    C. every 8 hours
    D. at the end of each trip

14. Except for the name and main address of the carrier, all entries relating to the driver's record of duty status must be   14.____

    A. printed in ink or typed   B. made by the carrier dispatcher
    C. made in front of a witness   D. in the driver's handwriting

15. Which of the following is NOT required to be put in a driver's record of duty status? 15.____

    A. Time spent in a sleeper berth
    B. Total hours in each duty status
    C. Origin and destination
    D. The name and make of the vehicle

16. If any emergency delays a run which could normally have been completed within hours 16.____
of service limits, the driver

    A. must still stop driving when the hours of service limits is reached
    B. may drive for 1 extra hour
    C. may drive for 2 extra hours
    D. may finish the run without violation

17. A driver declared *Out of Service* 17.____

    A. must take a road test before driving again
    B. must wait 72 hours before driving again
    C. must appeal to the Director of the Bureau of Motor Carrier Safety to drive
    D. can drive again only after hours of service requirements are met

18. If a vehicle on a trip is in a condition likely to cause an accident or breakdown, the driver 18.____
should

    A. report it at the end of the run so repairs can be made
    B. drive at lower speeds for the rest of the run
    C. stop immediately unless going on to the nearest repair shop is safer than stopping
    D. change the route so as to get away from heavily traveled roads

19. If authorized federal inspectors find a vehicle which is likely to cause an accident or 19.____
breakdown, it will be

    A. reported to the carrier for repair as soon as the vehicle is not scheduled
    B. reported to the carrier for repair at the end of the trip
    C. marked with an *out of service vehicle* sticker and not driven until repairs are made
    D. the driver will be held responsible and declared *out of service*

20. If the driver personally makes repairs on an *out of service* vehicle, the 20.____

    A. work must be approved by a mechanic
    B. driver must complete and sign a *Certification of Repairman* form
    C. work must be approved by a supervisor
    D. work must be approved by a federal inspector

21. Department of Transportation regulations covering the driving and parking of vehicles 21.____
containing hazardous materials

    A. replace state and local laws
    B. prevent states and cities from having their own laws
    C. must be obeyed even if state or local laws are less strict or disagree
    D. should not be obeyed if state or local laws disagree

22. A vehicle which contains hazardous materials other than Class A or B explosives must   22.____
be attended at all times by the

    A. driver
    B. driver, except when involved in other driver duties
    C. driver or a person chosen by the driver
    D. driver or a police officer

23. A vehicle containing Class A or B explosives or other hazardous materials on a trip is   23.____
attended

    A. when the person in charge is anywhere within 100 feet of the vehicle
    B. as long as the driver can see the vehicle from 200 feet away
    C. when the person in charge is within 100 feet and has a clear view of the vehicle
    D. when the person in charge is resting in the berth

24. Except for short periods when operations make it necessary, trucks carrying Class A or B   24.____
explosives cannot be parked any closer to bridges, tunnels, buildings or crowds of people
than _____ feet.

    A. 50   B. 100   C. 200   D. 300

25. Smoking or carrying a lighted cigarette, cigar, or pipe near a vehicle which contains   25.____
explosives, oxidizing or flammable materials is not allowed EXCEPT

    A. in the closed cab of the vehicle
    B. when the vehicle is moving
    C. at a distance of 25 feet or more from the vehicle
    D. when approved by the carrier

—————

KEY (CORRECT ANSWERS)

1.	B		11.	C
2.	B		12.	B
3.	C		13.	A
4.	D		14.	D
5.	C		15.	D
6.	B		16.	D
7.	A		17.	D
8.	C		18.	C
9.	C		19.	C
10.	B		20.	B

21.	C
22.	B
23.	C
24.	D
25.	C

———

EXAMINATION SECTION
TEST 1

DIRECTIONS: Each question or incomplete statement is followed by several suggested answers or completions. Select the one that BEST answers the question or completes the statement. *PRINT THE LETTER OF THE CORRECT ANSWER IN THE SPACE AT THE RIGHT.*

1. The state has set up a system of rigid controls for the licensing of drivers. The MAIN reason for these controls is to

   A.   insure that people using the highways carry proper identification
   B.   make sure that cars are regularly inspected to prevent accidents due to mechanical failure
   C.   maintain up-to-date records of the number of cars using the roads
   D.   protect the public from irresponsible and dangerous drivers

   1.____

2. A traffic regulation of the department of traffic states that the driver of any vehicle shall not turn such vehicle so as to proceed in the opposite direction upon any street in a business district.
   According to this regulation, you are prohibited from

   A.   making a *U* turn on any street
   B.   making a *U* turn on a street in the business district
   C.   backing your car to park on a business street
   D.   backing your car on any street where there is traffic

   2.____

3. Often, when parking regulations in an area are changed, it is the custom for the first day or two of the change to issue warnings to violators, rather than summonses.
   Of the following, the MAIN reason for issuing warnings rather than summonses is to

   A.   give motorists a chance to become acquainted with the new regulations
   B.   judge public reaction to the change
   C.   show the public that the new regulations will be strictly and impartially enforced
   D.   see if the new regulations will work

   3.____

4. Employees who deal with the public may sometimes be required to take an action, in accordance with the rules and regulations of their department, which may cause a citizen to become angry or resentful.
   In order to keep good public relations in such a situation, it would be MOST preferable for the employee to say to the citizen:

   A.   "My job is to uphold the rules and regulations even if you don't like them."
   B.   "Rules and regulations are made to be obeyed by everyone."
   C.   "Let me explain as best I can the reasons for my action."
   D.   "I'm only doing the job I'm getting paid for, so don't get mad at me."

   4.____

5. Assume that as a city employee on official business, you have parked a city vehicle at a metered parking space. When you come back later, you see a policeman writing out a summons and the red flag (parking time expired) shows on the parking meter.
   In this situation, you should

   5.____

A. point out to the policeman that the car's license plate shows that this is a city car
B. explain to the policeman in a polite manner that you are on city business and ask him not to give you the summons
C. accept the summons as you are obviously illegally parked
D. call your supervisor, explain what is going on, and ask him what you should do

6. One day, during the absence of your regular supervisor, your temporary supervisor assigns you to some work that you have done before but instructs you to do it a different way than you have done it in the past.
Of the following, it would be BEST for you to

6.____

A. do the work the way you have been doing it in the past since this is a better method
B. explain to your temporary supervisor the method you have used in the past
C. follow the instructions of your temporary supervisor without question
D. speak to other employees to see if they have been assigned to this work too and how they are doing it

7. The BEST reason for requiring employees to learn the rules and regulations of their jobs is to

7.____

A. help them do their work safely and correctly
B. prepare them for future promotion to higher positions
C. develop their study habits
D. test their alertness

8. Departments generally require that an employee who is ill and cannot report to work call his supervisor to tell him that he is ill.
Of the following, the BEST reason for having such a requirement is to make it possible for the supervisor to

8.____

A. keep an accurate record of absences
B. make plans, if necessary, to cover the work of the absent employee
C. call the absent employee back to make sure that he is really at home
D. mail important instructions to the absent employee

9. If you find that there isn't enough room on a required department form to include all the information you want to give, it would be BEST to

9.____

A. not use the form
B. write as much as will fit on the form and tell your supervisor orally about the rest of the information
C. leave out some of the less important information
D. attach another sheet with the additional information written on it

10. A *scofflaw* is a term applied to a person who has

10.____

A. accumulated many unanswered traffic summonses
B. his driver's license revoked by the state commissioner of motor vehicles
C. insufficient automobile liability insurance
D. failed to renew his driver's license but continues to drive a car

11. A flashing red traffic signal means 11.____

    A. stop and then proceed with caution
    B. slow down and proceed with caution
    C. street closed to traffic
    D. wait for green

12. Which one of the following shapes of road traffic signs would you LEAST expect to find in the city? 12.____

    A. ▽   B. ▭   C. ⬡   D. ◯

13. An intersection with a flashing yellow traffic signal means MOST NEARLY 13.____

    A. *Do Not Enter the Intersection*
    B. *Proceed with Caution*
    C. *Watch Out For Pedestrians Crossing*
    D. *Reduce Speed and Stop*

14. Suppose you are driving straight ahead at moderate speed on a two-way street and have entered an intersection when the traffic light facing you changes from green to red and green.
In this situation, it would be BEST for you to 14.____

    A. come to a stop
    B. back up out of the intersection
    C. blow your horn and speed up
    D. continue across the intersection

15. Peach Street is one-way northbound and is crossed by Apple Street which is one-way eastbound.
If there are no traffic or other directional signals at the intersection, it would be CORRECT to make a 15.____

    A. right turn from Apple Street into Peach Street
    B. left turn from Peach Street into Apple Street
    C. right turn from Peach Street into Apple Street
    D. left or right turn from either street if there is no cross traffic

16. You are driving a car. In front of you is a moving car with its trunk lid in the air.
Of the following, the CHIEF traffic hazard in this situation is the 16.____

    A. excessively slow precautionary driving speed of driver in front of you
    B. poor rear visibility for the driver in front of you
    C. poor visibility ahead for you
    D. possibility of some contents of the open trunk falling onto the roadway

17. If you have a blowout while driving at 50 miles an hour on an expressway, the BEST thing   17.____
for you to do is to

    A. steer the car at a sharp angle onto the shoulder of the road and coast to a stop
    B. put the car in low gear, turn off the ignition, and apply the brakes slowly
    C. turn off the ignition, put the car in neutral gear, and coast to a stop
    D. grip the steering wheel tightly to keep the car steady, let up on the gas pedal, and
       brake slowly

18. If you are driving a car with automatic transmission and the rear end of the car begins to   18.____
skid to the right, the BEST way to get out of the skid is to steer the car to the

    A. right, avoid any hard braking, and keep the car in *drive*
    B. left, pump the brake smoothly, and keep the car in *drive*
    C. right, pump the brake smoothly, and put the car in *neutral*
    D. left, avoid any hard braking, and put the car in *neutral*

19. Most cars have automatic chokes which help to start a cold engine.   19.____
  The choke performs this function by

    A. regulating battery current to produce a hot spark
    B. pre-heating the gasoline before it enters the engine
    C. reducing the amount of air going to the carburetor
    D. directing the current from the generator directly to the starting motor

20. Driving with a window open is recommended MAINLY in order to prevent the accumula-   20.____
tion inside the car of an excess of

    A. moisture
    B. carbon monoxide gas
    C. sulfur dioxide contaminants
    D. battery acid fumes

21. The MAIN reason for requiring cars to be parked parallel to and as close to a curb as   21.____
possible is to

    A. allow drivers to get out without stepping onto the roadway
    B. leave the greatest amount of space open for passing traffic
    C. provide parking space for the greatest number of cars
    D. reduce damage to parked cars

22. The MAIN purpose of extending the program of *alternate side of the street parking* to   22.____
many residential areas is to

    A. relieve traffic congestion
    B. make it easier to clean the streets
    C. reduce the number of traffic accidents
    D. reduce the number of cars parked on the streets overnight

30

23. The CHIEF reason for installing a *progressive system* of traffic lights on the main one-way streets in Manhattan is to   23.____

    A. reduce speeding
    B. speed up the loading and unloading of trucks
    C. reduce the volume of traffic using these streets
    D. move more traffic with less delay

Questions 24-35.

DIRECTIONS: The following is an accident report similar to those used by city departments for reporting accidents. Questions 24 to 35 are to be answered ONLY on the basis of the information contained in this accident report.

ACCIDENT REPORT

Date of Accident: April 12,---

Place of Accident: 17th Ave. & 22nd Street

Time of Accident: 10:15 A.M.

Date of Report: April 15,---Friday

City Vehicle
  Operator's Name: John Smith
  Title: Motor Vehicle Operator
  Badge, No.: 17-5427
  Operator License No.: S2874-7513-3984
  Vehicle Code No.: B7-8213
  License Plate No.: BK-4782
  Damage to Vehicle: Left front fender dented; broken left front headlight and parking light; windshield wipers not operating

Vehicle No. 2
  Operator's Name: James Jones
  Operator's Address: 427 E. 198th St.
  Operator's License No.: J0837 0882-7851
  Owner's Name: Michael Greene
  Owner's Address: 582 E. 92nd St.
  License Plate No.: 6Y-3916
  Damage to Vehicle: Left front bumper bent inward; broken left front headlight; grille broken in three places

DESCRIPTION OF ACCIDENT: I was driving on 17th Avenue, a southbound one-way street, and made a slow, wide turn west into 22nd Street, a two-way street, because a moving van was parked near the corner on 22nd Street. As I completed my turn, a station wagon going east on 22nd Street hit me. The driver of the station wagon said he put on his brakes but he skidded on some oil that was on the street. The driver of the van saw the accident from his cab and told me that the station wagon skidded as he put on his brakes. Patrolman Jack Reed, Badge No. 24578, who was at the southeast corner of the intersection, saw what happened and made some notes in his memo book.

Persons Injured - Names and Addresses. If none, state NONE.

Witnesses - Names and Addresses. If none, state NONE:
  Jack Reed, 33-47 83rd Drive
  Thomas Quinn, 527 Flatlands Avenue

            Report prepared by: John Smith
            Title: Motor Vehicle Operator

24. According to the report, the accident happened on

    A. Friday, between 6:00 A.M and 12:00 Noon
    B. Friday, between 12:00 Noon and 6:00 P.M.
    C. Tuesday, between 6:00 A.M. and 12:00 Noon
    D. Monday, between 12:00 Noon and 6:00 P.M.

24.____

25. Which one of the following numbers is part of the driver's license of the operator of the city vehicle?

    A. 3984   B. 5247   C. 4782   D. 7851

25.____

26. The address of the driver of the city vehicle is

    A. not given in the report   B. 427 E. 198th Street
    C. 582 E. 92nd Street   D. 33-47 83rd Drive

26.____

27. A section of the report that is NOT properly filled out is

    A. Witnesses   B. Description of Accident
    C. Persons Injured   D. Damage to Vehicle

27.____

28. According to the accident report, if the only witnesses were the patrolman and the van driver, then the van driver's name is

    A. Reed   B. Quinn   C. Jones   D. Greene

28.____

29. According to the report, the diagram that would BEST show where the cars collided and where the moving van( ) was parked at the time of the accident is

29.____

30. According to the information in the report, it would be MOST correct to say that Michael   30.____
Greene was

    A. the driver of the station wagon
    B. a passenger in the station wagon
    C. the owner of the moving van
    D. the owner of the station wagon

31. According to the information in the report, a factor which contributed to the accident was   31.____

    A. a slippery road condition
    B. bad brakes of one car
    C. obstructed view of traffic light caused by parked van
    D. windshield wipers on the city car not operating properly

32. When a driver makes a report such as this, it is MOST important that he   32.____

    A. print the information so that his supervisor can read it quickly
    B. keep it short because a long report makes it look as though he is hiding a mistake
       behind many words
    C. show clearly why the accident isn't his fault
    D. give all the facts accurately and completely

33. The first two letters or numbers in the vehicle code number indicate the type of vehicle.   33.____
Two letters indicate an 8 passenger-8 cylinder car; two numbers indicates a 6 passen-
ger-8 cylinder car; a letter followed by a number indicates a 6 passenger-6 cylinder car; a
number followed by a letter indicates an 8 cylinder station wagon.
The car involved in this accident is, therefore, a(n)

    A. 8 cylinder station wagon
    B. 6 passenger-6 cylinder car
    C. 6 passenger-8 cylinder car
    D. 8 passenger-8 cylinder car

34. From the information in the report, the driver of the city vehicle may have been partially at   34.____
fault because he

    A. appears to have begun his turn from the wrong lane
    B. appears to have entered the wrong lane of traffic
    C. did not blow his horn as he made the turn
    D. should have braked as he made the turn

35. What evidence is there in the report that the two vehicles collided in front, drivers' side?   35.____

    A. The description of the accident
    B. There is no such evidence
    C. The type of damage to the vehicles
    D. The van driver's statement

Questions 36-42.

DIRECTIONS: Answer Questions 36 to 42 ONLY according to the information given in the fol-
               lowing passage.

The parking meter was designed many years ago primarily as a mechanism to assist in reducing overtime parking at the curb, to increase parking turnover, and to facilitate enforcement of parking regulations. That the meter has accomplished these basic functions is attested to by its use in an increasing number of cities.

A recent survey of cities in the United States indicates that overtime parking was reduced 75% or more in 47% of the cities surveyed, and to a lesser degree in 43% of the cities surveyed, making a total of 90% of the cities surveyed where the parking meter was found to be effective in reducing overtime parking at the curb.

A side effect of the reduction in overtime parking is the increase in parking turnover. Approximately 89% of the places surveyed found meters useful in this respect. Meters also encourage even spacing of cars at the curb. Unmetered curb parking is often so irregular that it wastes space or makes parking and departure difficult.

The effectiveness of parking meters, in the final analysis, rests upon the enforcement of regulations by squads of enforcement agents who will diligently patrol the metered area. The task of checking parking time is made easier with meters since violations can be checked from a moving vehicle or by visual sightings of an agent on foot patrol, and the laborious process of chalking tires is greatly reduced. It is reported that, after meters have been installed, it takes on the average only 25% of the time formerly required to patrol the same area.

The fact that a parker activates a mechanism that immediately begins to count time, that will indicate exactly when the parking time has expired, and that will advertise such fact by showing a red flag, tends to make a parker more conscious of his parking responsibilities than the hit and miss system of possible detection by a patrolman.

36. According to the above passage, when the parking meter was introduced, one of its major purposes was NOT to   36._____

   A.   cut down overtime curb parking
   B.   make curb parking available to more parkers
   C.   bring in revenue from parking fees
   D.   make it easier to enforce parking regulations

37. In the cities surveyed, how effective was the installation of parking meters in cutting down overtime parking?   37._____

   A.   It was effective to some degree in all the cities surveyed.
   B.   It was ineffective in only one out of every ten cities surveyed.
   C.   It reduced overtime parking at least 75% in most cities surveyed.
   D.   There was only a small reduction in overtime parking in 43% of the cities surveyed.

38. When overtime parking is reduced by the installation of parking meters, an accompanying result is   38._____

   A.   an increase in the amount of parking space
   B.   the use of the available parking spaces by more cars
   C.   the faster movement of traffic
   D.   a decrease in the number of squads required to enforce traffic regulations

39. According to the above passage, on streets which have parking meters, as compared with streets which are unmetered,   39.____

    A. there is less waste of parking space
    B. parking is more difficult
    C. parking time limits are irregular
    D. drivers waste more time looking for an empty parking space

40. According to the above passage, the use of parking meters will NOT be effective unless   40.____

    A. parking areas are patrolled in automobiles
    B. it is combined with the chalking of tires
    C. the public cooperates
    D. there is strict enforcement of parking regulations

41. According to the above passage, one reason why there is greater compliance with parking regulations when parking time is regulated by meters rather than by a foot patrolman chalking tires is that   41.____

    A. overtime parking becomes glaringly evident to everyone
    B. the parker is himself responsible for operating the timing mechanism
    C. there is no personal relationship between parker and enforcing officer
    D. the timing of elapsed parking time is accurate

42. In the last paragraph of the above passage, the words *a parker activates a mechanism* refers to the fact that a motorist   42.____

    A. starts the timing device of the meter working
    B. parks his car
    C. checks whether the meter is working
    D. starts the engine of his car

Questions 43-45.

DIRECTIONS: Answer Questions 43 to 45 ONLY according to the information given in the following passage.

When markings upon the curb or the pavement of a street designate parking space, no person shall stand or park a vehicle in such designated parking space so that any part of such vehicle occupies more than one such space or protrudes beyond the markings designating such a space, except that a vehicle which is a size too large to be parked within a single designated parking space shall be parked with the front bumper at the front of the space with the rear of the vehicle extending as little as possible into the adjoining space to the rear, or vice-versa.

43. The regulation quoted above applies to parking at any   43.____

    A. curb or pavement
    B. metered spaces
    C. street where parking is permitted
    D. parking spaces with marked boundaries

44. The regulation quoted above prohibits the occupying of more than one indicated parking   44._____
space by

    A. any vehicle
    B. large vehicles
    C. small vehicles
    D. vehicles in spaces partially occupied

45. In the regulation quoted above, the term *vice-versa* refers to a vehicle of a size too large   45._____
parked with

    A. front bumper flush with front of parking space it occupies
    B. front of vehicle extending into front of parking space
    C. rear bumper flush with rear of parking space it occupies
    D. rear of vehicle protruding into adjoining parking space

---

KEY (CORRECT ANSWERS)

1.	D	11.	A	21.	B	31.	A	41.	A
2.	B	12.	D	22.	B	32.	D	42.	A
3.	A	13.	B	23.	D	33.	B	43.	D
4.	C	14.	D	24.	C	34.	B	44.	C
5.	C	15.	C	25.	A	35.	C	45.	C
6.	B	16.	B	26.	A	36.	C		
7.	A	17.	D	27.	C	37.	B		
8.	B	18.	A	28.	B	38.	B		
9.	D	19.	C	29.	D	39.	A		
10.	A	20.	B	30.	D	40.	D		

TEST 2

DIRECTIONS: Each question or incomplete statement is followed by several suggested answers or completions. Select the one that BEST answers the question or completes the statement. *PRINT THE LETTER OF THE CORRECT ANSWER IN THE SPACE AT THE RIGHT.*

Questions 1-3.

DIRECTIONS: Answer Questions 1 to 3 ONLY according to the information given in the following passage.

Driver's and pedestrians face additional traffic hazards during the fall months. Changing autumn weather conditions, longer hours of darkness, and the abrupt nightfall during the evening rush hour can mean more traffic deaths and injuries unless drivers and pedestrians exercise greater care and alertness. Drivers must adjust to changing light conditions; they cannot use the same driving habits and attitudes at dusk as they do during daylight. Moderate speed and continual alertness are imperative for safe driving at this time of year.

1. According to the above passage, two new traffic risks which motorists face in the fall are   1.____

    A. changing weather conditions and more traffic during the evening rush hour
    B. fewer hours of daylight and sudden nightfall
    C. less care by pedestrians and a change in autumn weather conditions
    D. more pedestrians on the street and longer hours of darkness

2. According to the above passage, there may be more traffic deaths and injuries in the fall   2.____
MAINLY because both pedestrians and drivers are

    A. distracted by car lights being turned on earlier
    B. hurrying to get home from work in the evening
    C. confronted with more traffic dangers
    D. using the streets in greater numbers

3. According to the above passage, an essential requirement of driving safely in the Fall is   3.____

    A. eyes down on the road at all times
    B. very slow speed
    C. no passing
    D. reasonable speed

Questions 4-6.

DIRECTIONS: Answer Questions 4 to 6 ONLY according to the information given in the following passage.

A traffic sign is a device mounted on a fixed or portable support through which a specific message is conveyed by means of words or symbols. It is erected by legal authority for the purpose of regulating, warning, or guiding traffic.

A regulatory sign is used to indicate the required method of traffic movement or the per-mitted use of a highway. It gives notice of traffic regulations that apply only at specific places or at specific times that would not otherwise be apparent.

A warning sign is used to call attention to conditions on or near a road that are actually or potentially hazardous to the safe movement of traffic.

A guide sign is used to direct traffic along a route or toward a destination, or to give directions, distances, or information concerning places or points of interest.

4. According to the above passage, which one of the following is NOT a *Regulatory* sign?　　4.____

    A. Right turn on red signal permitted
    B. Trucks use right lane
    C. Slippery when wet
    D. Speed limit 60

5. According to the above passage, which one of the following LEAST fits the description of　　5.____
   a *Warning* sign?

    A. No right turn
    B. Falling rock zone
    C. Low clearance 12 ft. 6 in.
    D. Merging traffic

6. According to the above passage, which one of the following messages is LEAST likely to　　6.____
   be conveyed by a *Guide* sign?

    A. South bound   B. Signal ahead
    C. Bridge next exit   D. Entering city

Questions 7-8.

DIRECTIONS: Answer Questions 7 and 8 ONLY according to the information given in the fol-lowing passage.

The State Vehicle and Traffic law provides for all new driving licenses to be issued on a six-month probationary basis. The probationary license will be cancelled if during this six-month period the driver is found guilty of tailgating, speeding, reckless driving, or driving while his ability is impaired by alcohol. The license will also be cancelled if the driver is found guilty of two other moving traffic violations. If a probationary license is cancelled, the driver must wait for sixty days after the date of cancellation before applying for another license, and if the application is approved, the applicant must meet certain additional requirements, including a new road test, before a new license will be issued.

7. It is MOST reasonable to assume that the main purpose of the law referred to above was　　7.____
   to

    A. find out who is responsible for most traffic accidents
    B. make the road tests more difficult for new drivers to pass
    C. make it harder to get a driver's license
    D. serve as a further check on the competence of new drivers

8. According to the above passage, we may assume that a probationary license will NOT 　8.____
be cancelled if a driver is found guilty of

    A. passing a red light and failing to keep to the right on a road
    B. following another vehicle too closely
    C. overtime parking at a meter on two or more occasions
    D. driving at 60 miles an hour on a road where the speed limit is 50 miles an hour

9. At a certain garage, there are 216 cars. Of these half are assigned to Department P, one- 　9.____
third to Department Q, one-ninth to Department R, and the rest to Department S.
How many cars are assigned to Department S?

    A. 9　　　　　　B. 12　　　　　　C. 18　　　　　　D. 24

10. In August a car travels 572 miles; in September, 438 miles; in October, 898 miles; and in 　10.____
December it travels 609 miles. If the five month average from August through December
was 673 miles traveled a month, then the number of miles traveled in November was

    A. 638　　　　　B. 706　　　　　C. 774　　　　　D. 848

11. Suppose the Units R, S, and T gave out a total of 1,715 parking tickets. 　11.____
If Unit R gave out twice as many tickets as Unit S, and Unit T gave out twice as many
tickets as Unit R, the number of tickets given out by Unit S is

    A. 270　　　　　B. 255　　　　　C. 245　　　　　D. 225

12. A car travels at the average rate of 40 miles an hour on the highway. 　12.____
If it takes 5 hours to make a trip of 150 miles, 2/3 of which is on the highway and the
rest on city streets, what was the average rate of speed of the car on city streets?

    A. 20　　　　　　B. 25　　　　　　C. 30　　　　　　D. 35

13. A motorist uses 27 gallons of gas on a trip of 351 miles. How many gallons of gas would 　13.____
he use if he took a trip of 624 miles under the same condition?

    A. 45　　　　　　B. 46　　　　　　C. 47　　　　　　D. 48

14. If the taxi rate in the city is $1.75 for the first 1/5 of a mile and 25¢ for each additional 1/5 　14.____
of a mile, a passenger whose fare was $4.75 traveled _____ miles.

    A. 2 1/5　　　　　B. 2 3/5　　　　　C. 3 2/5　　　　　D. 3 4/5

Questions 15-20.

DIRECTIONS: Answer Questions 15 to 20 ONLY according to the information given in the
              table below.

RIVER CITY - WEEKLY REPORT - WEEK ENDING 7/17				
	No. of Parking Meters		No. of Summonses Issued	
	On Streets	In Parking Lots	Overtime Parking	Other Violations
Zone P	840	1,680	460	130
Zone Q	1,400	420	1,200	480
Zone R	920	460	520	180
Zone S	1,550	620	800	200
Zone T	750	2,250	400	120

15. Compared to the total number of parking meters *On Streets,* the total number of parking meters *In Parking Lots* is   15._____

    A. 30 less   B. 60 less   C. 90 more   D. 30 more

16. Of all the summonses given out in Zone S during the week, what percent were for *other Violations?*   16._____

    A. 25   B. 20   C. 15   D. 5

17. The average number of summonses issued for overtime parking in each Zone during the week is MOST NEARLY   17._____

    A. 225   B. 340   C. 675   D. 1,090

18. Suppose that an employee can check 40 meters an hour on the streets and 3 times that number in a parking lot. If an employee works 7 hours a day, excluding a lunch period, and each meter is checked twice a day, how many employees must be assigned daily to Zone P to check all the meters?   18._____

    A. 7   B. 8   C. 10   D. 12

19. Suppose that a new parking lot is to be built in Zone Q. How many metered spaces must there be in this new parking lot so that Zone Q will have the same ratio of street meters to parking lot meters as Zone R?   19._____

    A. 700   B. 440   C. 350   D. 280

20. Comparing the total number of parking meters with the total number of summonses issued, it is CORRECT to state that the zone with the _____ number of meters issued the _____ number of summonses.   20._____

    A. smallest; smallest   B. largest; largest
    C. smallest; largest   D. largest; smallest

21. Of the following, the one which is NOT a part of the ignition system of an automobile is the   21._____

    A. battery   B. distributor
    C. master cylinder   D. spark plugs

22. Of the following, the BEST practice to follow when driving is to stay at least   22._____

    A. one car length behind the vehicle directly in front for each 20 miles per hour of speed of your own vehicle
    B. 20 feet behind the vehicle directly in front for each 10 miles per hour of speed of your own vehicle
    C. twice as far behind the vehicle directly in front on expressways as on city streets
    D. two car lengths behind the vehicle directly in front at any speed on city streets

23. When applied to a motor vehicle, the term *wheel alignment* USUALLY refers to the   23._____
adjustment of the _____ wheel(s).

    A. front   B. rear
    C. front and rear   D. steering

24. As an automobile makes a sharp turn, the rear wheel which is on the inside of the turn   24._____

    A. rotates at a faster speed than the outside rear wheel
    B. rotates at a slower speed than the outside rear wheel
    C. rotates at the same speed as the outside rear wheel
    D. slips slightly while the outside rear wheel does not slip

25. The MOST accurate of the following statements about driving and driving practices is   25._____
that

    A. an angry driver is more likely to have an accident than a calm driver
    B. high beam headlights penetrate fog better than low beam headlights
    C. letting air out of the tires greatly improves traction on snow
    D. wearing tinted glasses makes night driving safer by reducing the light from oncoming vehicles

26. In driving, you hear a fire siren behind you.   26._____
The procedure to follow is

    A. decrease your speed slowly, coming to a full stop
    B. increase your speed to keep well ahead of the fire apparatus
    C. pull over to the right as far as possible and stop
    D. turn off at the first available intersection

27. When you are approaching an intersection with the lights, you see another vehicle travel-   27._____
ing against the lights about to cross your path.
The PROPER thing for you to do is

    A. call a traffic policeman at once and tell him the situation
    B. continue on your way even if an accident should occur since you have the right of way
    C. give the proper signal and stop immediately
    D. sound your horn and shout to the other driver to clear the road

28. The tail light of a passenger car MUST be visible at night for a distance of _____ feet.   28._____

    A. 350   B. 400   C. 450   D. 500

29. The headlights of a passenger car MUST be able to show up objects at a distance of _____ feet.

    A. 350   B. 400   C. 450   D. 500

29._____

30. A broken white line on a city street indicates

    A. separate traffic lanes which may be crossed if they do not interfere with traffic
    B. no crossing from the solid line side of the road but crossing is allowed from the broken line side with proper caution
    C. separate opposing traffic lanes where no crossing is allowed
    D. separate opposing traffic lanes where crossing is allowed under favorable conditions

30._____

31. A solid and broken line indicates

    A. separate traffic lanes which may be crossed if they do not interfere with traffic
    B. no crossing from the solid line side of the road but crossing is allowed from the broken line side with proper caution
    C. separate opposing traffic lanes where no crossing is allowed
    D. separate opposing traffic lanes where crossing is allowed under favorable conditions

31._____

32. A double solid line indicates

    A. separate traffic lanes which may be crossed if they do not interfere with traffic
    B. no crossing from the solid line side of the road but crossing is allowed from the broken line side with proper caution
    C. separate opposing traffic lanes where no crossing is allowed
    D. separate opposing traffic lanes where crossing is allowed under favorable conditions

32._____

33. The BEST reason for NOT passing another car when going up a hill is that

    A. the car you are passing is being slowed down by the steepness of the grade
    B. the strain of speeding up your car may damage your engine
    C. you can't get the additional speed while climbing a hill
    D. you can't see beyond the crest while climbing it

33._____

34. The BEST reason for driving slowly when approaching a busy intersection is that

    A. a bus stop is frequently found at a busy intersection
    B. busy intersections provide more opportunity for accidents
    C. a policeman is assigned to regulate traffic at such an intersection
    D. traffic controls must be observed

34._____

35. While waiting in traffic for a red light to change, the PROPER procedure is to

    A. pull up your handbrake and move over to the curb
    B. put your gears into neutral ready to shift into low
    C. race your motor to be sure it doesn't stall
    D. turn off your ignition while keeping the foot brake on

35._____

36. If a driver loses his operator's license, the PROPER procedure is to   36.____

    A. apply for a new license
    B. drive without a license until it is time to renew the lost one
    C. get a letter from the police department explaining the entire situation
    D. use a friend's license when he must drive

37. If the accelerator on a car you are driving fails to shut off while the car is in motion after   37.____
you have removed your foot from the pedal, you should

    A. blow your horn to warn vehicles and pedestrians in front of you to clear the road
    B. call a patrolman to give you assistance
    C. drive to the garage for expert help
    D. release the clutch and turn off the ignition immediately

38. Shock, a condition often brought on by a serious injury to any part of the body, is danger-   38.____
ous MAINLY because

    A. body temperature rises too high
    B. blood pressure becomes very high
    C. the injured person remains unconscious for a long time
    D. there is a reduction in the flow of blood to the vital organs

39. If a little *battery fluid* accidentally gets into a person's eye, the FIRST thing to do is to   39.____

    A. call a doctor or ambulance
    B. find out what safety rule was broken
    C. put several drops of clean olive oil in the eye
    D. wash the eye with large quantities of plain water

40. If an unconscious person is found on the sidewalk, the BEST of the following to do right   40.____
away is to

    A. cover him to keep him warm
    B. give him sips of hot tea or coffee
    C. move him into the nearest building
    D. shake him gently to arouse him

41. To keep germs from entering a wound, it is BEST to   41.____

    A. apply a sterilized dressing to the wound
    B. put an antiseptic on the wound
    C. squeeze the wound gently to make it bleed
    D. wash the wound with soap and hot water

42. If several persons are injured in an accident, the one who should be treated FIRST is the   42.____
person who

    A. has a compound fracture   B. has severe burns
    C. is bleeding seriously   D. is in the greatest pain

43. Suppose that a car ran a total of 9,888 miles in a four month period from September through December, inclusive. It used 234 gallons of gas in September, 203 gallons in October, 191 gallons in November, and 196 gallons in December.
The average number of miles it traveled per gallon of gasoline was

43.____

   A. 10   B. 11   C. 12   D. 12 1/2

44. A government agency has a policy of replacing 1/3 of its vehicles each year. Of the twenty vehicles the agency is requesting in the budget, 95% are replacements.
If the request is granted, the total number of vehicles in the agency will be

44.____

   A. 19   B. 27   C. 58   D. 61

45. Car A averaged 21 miles to a gallon of gas. Car B averaged 18 miles to a gallon of gas. Each car used 14 gallons of gas.
Car A traveled _____ miles more than Car B.

45.____

   A. 42   B. 39   C. 28   D. 14

46. A garage has a gas tank with a capacity of 500 gallons. During the week, 210 gallons were used, and 340 gallons were delivered at the end of the week to fill the tank. How many gallons of gas were in the tank at the beginning of the week?

46.____

   A. 160   B. 210   C. 340   D. 370

47. The list price of Vehicle A is $42,000 and that of Vehicle B is $38,000. The city can get a discount of 20% of the list price on Vehicle A and 10% of the list price on Vehicle B. How much cheaper can the city buy Vehicle A than Vehicle B?

47.____

   A. $200   B. $600   C. $2,000   D. $6,000

48. In a certain bureau, there are four employees who each earn $250 a month, twelve employees who each earn $300 a month, and two employees who each earn $350 a month. The monthly payroll for all these employees is

48.____

   A. $4,900   B. $5,100   C. $5,300   D. $5,500

49. If the average passenger car needs 120 square feet of parking space, the LARGEST number of such cars that could be parked in a garage with a usable floor area that measures 70 feet by 100 feet is

49.____

   A. 52   B. 54   C. 56   D. 58

50. On a certain bridge, the toll for a motorcycle is 5/7 the toll for a passenger car, and 1/3 the toll for a truck.
If the toll for a passenger car is $1.75, then the toll for a truck on this bridge is

50.____

   A. $2.50   B. $3.75   C. $5.00   D. $6.25

KEY (CORRECT ANSWERS)

1.	B	11.	C	21.	C	31.	B	41.	C
2.	C	12.	A	22.	B	32.	C	42.	C
3.	D	13.	D	23.	A	33.	D	43.	C
4.	C	14.	B	24.	B	34.	B	44.	C
5.	A	15.	A	25.	A	35.	B	45.	A
6.	B	16.	B	26.	C	36.	A	46.	D
7.	D	17.	C	27.	C	37.	D	47.	B
8.	C	18.	C	28.	D	38.	B	48.	C
9.	B	19.	D	29.	A	39.	D	49.	D
10.	D	20.	D	30.	A	40.	D	50.	B

TEST 3

DIRECTIONS: Each question or incomplete statement is followed by several suggested answers or completions. Select the one that BEST answers the question or completes the statement. *PRINT THE LETTER OF THE CORRECT ANSWER IN THE SPACE AT THE RIGHT.*

1. To straighten out a car in which the rear wheels have started to skid to the right, the recommended procedure is for the driver to steer to the   1.____

    A. left, take the car out of gear, and apply the brakes gently
    B. right, ease up on the accelerator pedal, and apply the brakes firmly
    C. left, ease up on the accelerator pedal, and avoid braking
    D. right, ease up on the accelerator pedal, and avoid braking

2. When driving in heavy traffic for a long distance on a four lane one-way avenue, it is good driving practice to   2.____

    A. drive in the left lane
    B. drive in the middle lanes
    C. drive in the right lane
    D. change from one lane to another from time to time

3. According to the state vehicle and traffic law and good driving practice, the distance between wheels and curb when a car is parked parallel to the curb should be NO more than _____ inches.   3.____

    A. 12   B. 10   C. 8   D. 6

4. Poor driving is indicated when a driver   4.____

    A. gives up the right of way to allow another car to enter a stream of traffic in front of him
    B. positions his car so as to prevent a possible accident to a following car unable to see the danger
    C. in his desire to be careful, drives slowly in both the right-hand lane and in the passing lane
    D. frequently gives up the right of way to show his courtesy

Questions 5-6.

DIRECTIONS: Questions 5 and 6 are based on the information contained in the following paragraph.

Many experiments have been made on the effects of alcoholic beverages. These studies show that alcohol decreases alertness and efficiency. It decreases self-consciousness and, at the same time, increases confidence and feelings of ease and relaxation. It impairs attention and judgment. It destroys fear of consequences. Usual cautions are thrown to the winds. Habit systems become disorganized. The driver who uses alcohol tends to disregard his usual safety practices. He may not even be aware that he is disregarding them. His reaction time slows down; normally quick reactions are not possible for him. To make matters worse, he may not realize he is slower. His eye muscles may be so affected that his vision is not normal. He cannot correctly judge the speed of his car or of any other car. He cannot correctly estimate distances being covered by each. He becomes a highway menace.

5. The paragraph states that the drinking of alcohol makes a driver   5.____

    A. more alert   B. less confident
    C. more efficient   D. less attentive

6. From the above paragraph, it is reasonable to assume that a driver may overcome the   6.____
bad effects of drinking alcohol by

    A. being more cautious
    B. relying on his good driving habits to a greater extent than normally
    C. watching the road more carefully
    D. waiting for the alcohol to wear off before driving

7. For better driving effectiveness on snowy and icy streets in winter driving, it is BEST to   7.____
drive as usual but with

    A. slower speeds and without sudden speed or direction change
    B. slightly deflated tires for better traction
    C. tighter brakes than usual to permit more positive stops
    D. tighter steering than usual to give more positive control

8. In night driving, when passing oncoming cars that have bright headlights, it is wise to   8.____

    A. use colored glasses to help cut down the glare
    B. slow down and fix your eyes on the right-hand side of the road to cut down the
        glare
    C. speed up so as to pass quickly and reduce the effect of the glare
    D. switch on your high beam lights to see clearly enough to pass safely

9. When making a left turn from a one-way street into a one-way avenue, you should   9.____
approach the turn in the

    A. left lane of the street and turn so as to leave the intersection in the left lane of the
        avenue
    B. right lane of the street and turn so as to leave the intersection in the left lane of the
        avenue
    C. right lane of the street and turn so as to leave the intersection in the lane to the
        right of the middle of the avenue
    D. left lane of the street and turn so as to leave the intersection in the lane to the right
        of the middle of the avenue

10. According to good driving practice, the MINIMUM distance for signaling your intention to   10.____
make a turn is _____ feet.

    A. 20   B. 40   C. 70   D. 100

11. When a tire blows out while you are driving, the recommended procedure for stopping   11.____
safely is to grip the steering wheel hard to control the car, let up on the accelerator, and

    A. put the car into neutral and apply a firm hard pressure on the brake pedal
    B. keep the car in gear and apply a firm hard pressure on the brake pedal
    C. keep the car in gear and apply the brakes very gently and slowly
    D. put the car into neutral and apply the brakes very gently and slowly

12. When a hand signal is used by a driver to indicate a stop or a decrease in speed of his vehicle, the hand and arm should be extended   12.____

   A. horizontally with palm forward
   B. horizontally with palm down
   C. upward
   D. downward

13. You are driving north on the East River Drive and as you start around a curve, you see that something has happened ahead, and all northbound traffic has come to a stop about 300 feet ahead of you.   13.____
You should

   A. step hard on the brake to stop your car immediately
   B. maintain your speed, roll down your window, extend your arm, and wave it as a warning to the drivers behind you
   C. maintain your speed and make a quick stop when you reach the line of cars if they are still stopped
   D. pump your brake pedal and bring your car to a stop slowly

14. The MOST serious result of driving through flooded sections of streets or highways is USUALLY   14.____

   A. wet brakes   B. a wet exhaust system
   C. a wet master cylinder   D. a wet intake manifold

15. When you have to drive at night in a dense fog, it is MOST desirable to drive   15.____

   A. slowly, using the low beam of the headlights
   B. slowly, using parking lights only
   C. slowly, using the high beam of the headlights
   D. very slowly, using the high beam of the headlights and blowing your horn steadily

16. The length of roadway needed by the average driver when stopping in a hurry from a speed of 60 miles per hour while traveling on a superhighway is MOST NEARLY _____ feet.   16.____

   A. 150   B. 60   C. 300   D. 200

17. Driving with a car window partly open at all times, regardless of the weather or season of the year, is advisable MAINLY to   17.____

   A. maintain a reasonable car temperature
   B. prevent fogging of the car windows
   C. permit the escape of unpleasant odors from the interior
   D. maintain proper ventilation of the interior

18. When using an acceleration lane to enter a main traffic lane of a highway on which the speed limit is 60 miles per hour, it is DESIRABLE to

    A.   enter the main traffic lane at the speed of the vehicles using the main traffic lane
    B.   enter the main traffic lane at about one-half the speed of the vehicles using the main traffic lane
    C.   enter the main traffic lane slowly but without stopping
    D.   come to a complete stop before entering the main traffic lane

18.____

19. You are driving at the speed limit on a four-lane one-way avenue, and a driver behind you sounds his horn and starts to pass you.
The PROPER procedure for you to follow is to

    A.   block him to keep him from exceeding the speed limit
    B.   let him pass and overtake him later
    C.   decrease your speed slightly and let him go by
    D.   increase your speed so as to get out of his way

19.____

20. Driving at night is more dangerous than driving in the daytime because

    A.   there are more cars on the road at night
    B.   visibility is poorer at night than during the day
    C.   drunken drivers are more numerous
    D.   most drivers drive faster at night than during the day

20.____

21. A manufacturer recommends a tire pressure of 26 pounds for a certain tire.
For a LONGEST life and even tread wear, it is desirable to use an actual tire pressure of _____ pounds.

    A. 23   B. 26   C. 30   D. 35

21.____

22. If brakes squeak when they are being applied, the MOST probable cause is

    A.   worn brake linings
    B.   improperly lubricated brake linings
    C.   too little brake fluid in the system
    D.   a stiff master cylinder piston

22.____

23. When you pull off the road to investigate trouble with your engine, you must be careful not to touch the exhaust manifold because you may

    A.   upset the engine timing
    B.   upset the air-fuel ratio
    C.   get a severe electrical shock
    D.   get a severe burn

23.____

24. The liquid level in an automobile storage battery should always be above the plates.
It is good practice, however, to maintain the liquid level in the battery at a

    A.   low level throughout the year - just above the plates
    B.   higher level in the summer than in winter
    C.   up to the very top throughout the year
    D.   higher level in the winter than in summer

24.____

25. *Shimmy* of the front wheels of an automobile USUALLY occurs as a result of   25.____

    A.   tire unbalance   B.   over-lubricated wheel bearings
    C.   a broken shock absorber   D.   a broken front spring

26. After starting an engine in cold weather, to warm it up as fast as possible with least harm,   26.____
the BEST of the following techniques would be to

    A.   pump the accelerator pedal up and down for about a minute before driving off at
normal speed
    B.   hold down the accelerator steadily for about 10 seconds before driving off at nor-
mal speed
    C.   let the engine idle normally for about a minute before driving off at normal speed
    D.   let the engine idle normally for about a minute before driving off at slow speed

27. The MAIN purpose of a carburetor is to   27.____

    A.   keep the engine from overheating
    B.   cool the engine oil
    C.   control the circulation of cooling water
    D.   mix gasoline with air

28. A driver should understand the term *right of way* to be the   28.____

    A.   description of any roadway
    B.   description of the extreme right-hand lane of any roadway
    C.   privilege of passing a slower driver on the right of the roadway
    D.   privilege of the immediate use of the roadway

29. The horn on a motor vehicle is being used properly when it is sounded to   29.____

    A.   hasten the movement of slowly moving traffic at an intersection
    B.   indicate to the driver behind you that you wish to pass
    C.   warn a pedestrian of possible danger
    D.   clear a crosswalk of pedestrians so as to permit the turning of cars on a green light

30. When you leave your vehicle unattended while it is parked in a proper parking place, it is   30.____
legal to have the engine

    A.   running with the transmission lever in neutral as long as the brake is set
    B.   stopped with the key in the ignition lock and without the brake set as long as the
car is in reverse gear
    C.   stopped, the ignition locked by removal of the ignition key, the brake set, and the
car windows open
    D.   stopped, the ignition locked by removal of the ignition key, the car in reverse gear
instead of set brakes, and all windows closed with all doors locked

31. If you are driving south, in a business district, on a two-way avenue and you wish to   31.____
make a turn to go back north on the same avenue, the PROPER way to make the turn is
to

    A.   drive around a block and turn north into the avenue
    B.   keep to the right, back into a one-way west street, and then turn north into the ave-
nue

C.   keep to the center of the avenue, turn left into a one-way east street, back into the avenue heading north
D.   wait until the flow of traffic permits, and then make a simple U-turn

32.   In the city, when the use of lights is required while driving any motor vehicle other than an authorized emergency vehicle, it is illegal to use   32.____

A.   white parking lights
B.   low beam white headlights
C.   low beam yellow headlights
D.   white or yellow multiple beam headlights

33.   A properly posted *Play Street* sign indicates that the street is   33.____

A.   closed to all vehicular traffic
B.   closed to all vehicular traffic except to those drivers who have business or who reside on the street
C.   open to all traffic, but extreme caution is to be used in driving
D.   open to passenger vehicles but not to trucks

34.   Except where official signs indicate a different maximum speed limit, the speed limit in the city is _____ miles per hour.   34.____

A.   25   B.   28   C.   30   D.   35

35.   Parking regulations are being violated in a parking meter space during the hours in which the posted parking meter regulations are in force if   35.____

A.   upon parking, a coin is not deposited because of an unexpired time interval still showing on the meter
B.   after parking and depositing a coin, a second coin is deposited later to extend the period of parking the car
C.   a large commercial vehicle occupies more than a single parking space and a coin has been deposited only in the forward meter
D.   a coin has been properly deposited, but the car has been parked for the purpose of changing a tire

36.   While driving on a one-way street, you find that you must stop because a large moving van is blocking the way while the driver is jockeying the vehicle back and forth in order to park it. Cars accumulate behind you, and the drivers begin blowing their horns.
You should   36.____

A.   start blowing your horn in the hope of attracting a policeman
B.   get out of the car and look for a policeman to clear the traffic jam
C.   signal to the cars in back of you to back up so that all cars can back out of the street
D.   wait until there is sufficient clearance to drive safely past the van

37.   You are returning to the garage after having dropped a passenger off near his office. The passenger and his office are well known to you since you frequently drive him about the city. You suddenly discover that he forgot his glasses on the seat of the car.
You should   37.____

A.   telephone him to tell him that his glasses have been found and can be picked up at the garage
B.   hold on to the glasses so that you can return them the next time you drive him

    C.   drive on and turn the glasses in at the garage

    D.   drive right back to his office to give him the glasses

38.   You have left the garage and have stopped at your first place of call to pick up a passen-   38.____
ger. On opening the car door for him, you see a briefcase on the floor of the car.
You should

    A.   excuse yourself and return immediately to the garage with the briefcase

    B.   telephone your dispatcher as soon as you can and tell him what you found

    C.   open the briefcase as soon as you can to find out who owns it so that you can
return it

    D.   be patient and wait until you return to the garage at the end of the day to turn the
briefcase in

39.   You have been sent to a city office to pick up an important package. When you arrive at   39.____
9:30 A.M., you learn that the only person authorized to give you the package will not be
in until noon.
You should

    A.   return to the garage immediately

    B.   try to talk someone else into giving you the package

    C.   telephone your dispatcher immediately

    D.   wait for the authorized person to arrive

40.   A dispatcher gives you instructions to travel a certain route in an assignment with a strict   40.____
time schedule. You know that a large emergency excavation is causing long delays on
the route.
You should

    A.   tell the dispatcher about the probable delay

    B.   choose a different route which will get you to your destination on time

    C.   follow the given route and attempt to make up time before and after the delay

    D.   follow the given route and explain why you were late at your destination

41.   You have driven a city executive to a meeting in the morning, and you have to wait a half-   41.____
hour for him to come out to drive him to his next appointment. Parking is permitted in the
area but there is no open space available except by a fire hydrant.
Of the following, the BEST thing for you to do is to

    A.   double park, remain in the driver's seat, and keep the motor running

    B.   park by the hydrant, remain in the driver's seat, and keep the motor running

    C.   park by the hydrant, remain in the driver's seat, and shut the motor off

    D.   park by the hydrant, shut the motor off, get out of the car but remain in the immedi-
ate vicinity

42.   Upon the complete loss of oil pressure while a car is in operation, it is BEST that the car   42.____
be

    A.   pulled over to the side of the road and the engine stopped immediately for inspec-
tion

    B.   pulled over to the side of the road, and a repair truck called to install a new oil
pump

    C.   driven four miles to the department repair shop for inspection and repair

    D.   driven on its usual rounds and the incident reported to the department garage at
the end of the day

43. If the *charge and discharge* indicator, whether a meter or a light, suddenly indicates *discharge* while a car is in normal operation, it is BEST that the car be   43.____

    A. stopped immediately and then be towed to the department repair shop for repairs
    B. stopped immediately and a repair truck called to install a new battery
    C. drive on its usual rounds and the incident reported to the department garage at the end of the day
    D. drive four miles to the department repair shop for inspection and repair

44. The causes of MOST automobile accidents can be traced to   44.____

    A. heavy traffic conditions
    B. mistakes made by drivers
    C. mechanical failure of vehicles
    D. bad weather conditions

45. While you are driving a city official, you see a car up ahead suddenly swerve sharply to the right, climb the sidewalk, and crash into a store front. As your car is slowed, you see a crowd gather, and you notice that a policeman appears.
    You should   45.____

    A. pull over and help get the injured driver out of his car
    B. get the attention of the policeman and tell him who was at fault
    C. copy the car's license number
    D. drive on to your destination

Questions 46-50.

DIRECTIONS: Questions 46 to 50 are to answered ONLY on the basis of the information contained in the following accident report.

REPORT OF ACCIDENT

Date of Accident: Nov. 27 --- Time: 2:20 P.M. Date of Report: 11/28

Department Vehicle
Operator's Name: John Doe
Title: Motor Vehicle Operator
Vehicle Code No.: 17-129
License Plate No.: IN-2345
Damage to Vehicle: Crumpled
and torn front left fender,
broken left headlight, front
bumper bent outward on left
side, left front hubcap dented
badly and torn off.

Vehicle No. 2
Operator's Name: Richard Roe
Operator's Address: 983 E. 84 St.
Owner's Name: Robert Roe
Owner's Address: 983 E. 84 St.
License Plate No.: 9Y-8765
Damage to Vehicle: Crumped right
front fender, broken right head-
light and parking light, right
side of front bumper badly bent.

Place of Accident: 71st & 3rd Ave.

Description of Accident: I was driving west on 71st Street and started to turn north into 3rd Avenue since the light was still green for me. I stopped at the crosswalk because a woman was in the middle of 3rd Avenue crossing from west to east. She had just cleared my car when a Ford sedan, going north, crashed into my left front fender. The light was green on 3rd Avenue when he hit me. The woman who had crossed the avenue in front of me, and whose name I got as a witness, was standing on the corner when I got out of the car.

Persons Injured

_____   _____

_____   _____

Mrs. Mary Brown   Witness   215 E. 71st Street
                                      Report prepared by John Doe
                                      Title: Motor Vehicle Operator
                                      Badge # 17832

46. According to the description of the accident, the diagram that would BEST show how and where the vehicles crashed and the position of the witness (X) is   46.____

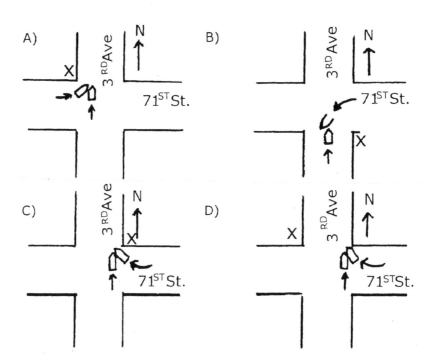

47. The pedestrian mentioned in the description of the accident was   47.____

     A. an unknown woman   B. Mary Brown
     C. an unknown man   D. Robert Roe

48. According to the information in the report, the one of the following statements which is   48.____
INCORRECT is

     A. both cars were moving when the accident happened
     B. one car was moving when the accident happened
     C. the department car was headed northwest when the accident happened
     D. the traffic lights had changed just before the accident happened

49. From the description of the accident as given in the report, the accident would PROBA-   49.____
BLY be classified as

     A. premeditated   B. calamitous
     C. minor   D. fatal

50. From a reading of the accident report, it can be seen that   50.____

     A. the witness was completely unfamiliar with the neighborhood in which the accident
       took place
     B. the accident occurred in the early hours of the morning
     C. neither driver owned the vehicle he was driving
     D. it was raining when the accident took place

———————

KEY (CORRECT ANSWERS)

1.	D	11.	C	21.	B	31.	A	41.	C
2.	B	12.	D	22.	A	32.	A	42.	A
3.	A	13.	D	23.	D	33.	B	43.	D
4.	C	14.	A	24.	B	34.	A	44.	B
5.	D	15.	A	25.	A	35.	B	45.	D
6.	D	16.	C	26.	D	36.	D	46.	C
7.	A	17.	D	27.	D	37.	D	47.	B
8.	B	18.	A	28.	D	38.	B	48.	A
9.	A	19.	C	29.	C	39.	C	49.	C
10.	D	20.	B	30.	C	40.	A	50.	C

———————

EXAMINATION SECTION
TEST 1

DIRECTIONS: Each question or incomplete statement is followed by several suggested answers or completions. Select the one that BEST answers the question or completes the statement. *PRINT THE LETTER OF THE CORRECT ANSWER IN THE SPACE AT THE RIGHT.*

Questions 1-5.

DIRECTIONS: Questions 1 to 5 are to be answered ONLY on the basis of information given in the following statement.

Fatigue can make a driver incompetent. He may become less vigilant. He may lose judgment as to the speed and distance of other cars. His reaction time is likely to be slowed down, and he is less able to resist glare. With increasing fatigue, driving efficiency falls. Finally, nodding at the wheel results, from which accidents follow almost invariably.

Accidents that occur with the driver asleep at the wheel are generally very serious. With the driver unconscious, no effort is made either to prevent the accident or to lessen its seriousness. Accidents increase as day wears on and reach their peak in the early evening and during the first half of the night. Driver fatigue undoubtedly plays a significant part in causing these frequent night accidents.

1. Among the results of fatigue, the statement does NOT indicate   1._____

    A. lessened hearing effectiveness
    B. lessened vigilance
    C. loss of driving efficiency
    D. increased reaction time

2. According to the statement, accidents almost always follow as a result of   2._____

    A. fatigue
    B. slowed down reaction time
    C. nodding at the wheel
    D. lessened vigilance

3. According to the statement, accidents that occur in the early evening and during the first   3._____
    half of the night are

    A. always caused by driver fatigue
    B. very frequently the result of lessened resistance to glare
    C. usually due to falling asleep at the wheel
    D. more frequent than accidents in the afternoon

4. According to the statement, very serious accidents result from   4._____

    A. falling asleep at the wheel
    B. poor driving
    C. lack of judgment
    D. poor vision

5. Referring to the statement, which of the following conclusions is NOT correct?   5.____

    A. There are only two paragraphs in the entire statement.
    B. One paragraph contains four sentences.
    C. There are six words in the first sentence.
    D. There is no sentence of less than six words.

Questions 6-8.

DIRECTIONS: Questions 6 to 8 are to be answered ONLY on the basis of the information contained in the following chart.

CHART "A"
Mileage between New York and points in Nearby Connecticut

	New York	Bridge-port	Dan-bury	Hart-ford	New Haven	New London	Stam-ford	Water-bury
New York	--	61	66	115	80	132	39	91
Bridgeport	61	--	27	54	19	71	22	30
Danbury	66	27	--	57	33	85	31	30
Hartford	115	54	57	--	37	44	76	27
New Haven	80	19	33	37	--	52	41	21
New London	132	71	85	44	52	--	93	62
Stamford	39	22	31	76	41	93	--	52
Waterbury	91	30	30	27	21	62	52	--

6. According to Chart "A", the total mileage on a continuous trip from New York to Danbury, to Waterbury, to New London, to New York would be _____ miles.   6.____

    A. 280   B. 290   C. 316   D. 294

7. According to Chart "A", the mileage between New Haven and New London is the same as the mileage between   7.____

    A. Danbury and Hartford   B. Hartford and New London
    C. Stamford and New Haven   D. Waterbury and Stamford

8. According to Chart "A", which of the following pairs of cities are CLOSEST to each other?   8.____

    A. Bridgeport and Hartford   B. New York and Bridgeport
    C. Hartford and Danbury   D. New Haven and New London

9. If you drove a car for three quarters of an hour and kept it at a steady speed of 30 miles per hour for half an hour, and a steady speed of 40 miles per hour the rest of the time, you would have traveled _____ miles.   9.____

    A. 20   B. 25   C. 30   D. 35

10. The length of curb available for the parking of cars on a certain street is 435 feet on the south side and 405 feet on the north side. Assuming that the bumper to bumper length of the average car to be parked is 15 feet, the total number of cars that can be parked bumper to bumper on both sides of the street will be   10.____

    A. 56   B. 58   C. 60   D. 61

11. If the charges against a certain vehicle total $2,000 a year, and 74%,of this is for repairs and maintenance, then the annual cost of repairs and maintenance for that vehicle is   11.____

    A. $50   B. $100   C. $150   D. $300

12. The list price of truck A is $13,500 and that of truck B is $12,000. If the discount on truck A is 20% and the discount on truck B is 10%, how much cheaper would it be to buy truck A instead of truck B? _____ cheaper.   12.____

    A. $900   B. $450   C. $400   D. no

13. There are three garages located in a single block. Garage A has 3/4 of the capacity of Garage B and 2/3 of the capacity of Garage C. If 88 cars can be parked in Garage B, the total number of cars that can be parked in all of the three garages is   13.____

    A. 186   B. 205   C. 238   D. 253

14. The city purchases 5 vehicles costing $6,000 each, 3 vehicles costing $8,000 each, and 2 vehicles costing $13,000 each.
The total cost of these vehicles is   14.____

    A. $67,000   B. $26,000   C. $80,000   D. $84,000

15. A car that averages 15 miles per gallon of gas is driven 135 miles. The gas tank is then filled to capacity by pumping in 12 gallons of gas. If the gas tank holds 18 gallons when full, the amount of gas in the tank at the beginning of the 135 mile trip must have been _____ gallons.   15.____

    A. 6   B. 9   C. 12   D. 15

16. The PROPER way to make a right turn from a two-way road into a one-way road is shown in Diagram   16.____

    A.   B.

    C.   D.

17. Traffic signs have standard shapes for certain types of information.　　　　17.＿＿＿

For instance, a round sign 🚦 indicat'es a railroad crossing

The shape of signs giving general traffic information, such as "No Parking" and "Do Not Enter", is USUALLY

A. Rectangular

B. Octagona

C. Triangular

D. Diamond

18. The so-called "blind spot" in motor vehicle operation refers to the region　　　　18.＿＿＿

 A. to the left of the driver where vision is obstructed by the left car pillar
 B. immediately to the right of the driver where vision is obstructed by the right car pillar
 C. immediately to the rear right of the car
 D. immediately to the rear left of the car

19. The MOST desirable manner of driving around a curve on a highway is to　　　　19.＿＿＿

 A. slow the car down before reaching the curve, start around the curve, and accelerate just before entering the straight-away
 B. accelerate at the start of the curve and slow down just before entering the straight-away
 C. start into the curve at normal straight-away speed and apply the brakes if necessary
 D. slow the car down before reaching the curve, put the car into neutral, and coast around the curve

20. At a speed of 40 miles per hour, a driver is NOT considered to be "tailgating" (following　　　20.＿＿＿
too closely) until the distance between his car and the car he is following is less than
＿＿＿＿ feet.

 A. 120   B. 60   C. 30   D. 0

21. You are driving alongside and to the rear of a large truck or bus as you approach and　　　21.＿＿＿
pass through an intersection. It is GOOD driving practice to

 A. accelerate   B. stay alongside
 C. blow your horn   D. stop

22. In approaching a traffic light such as the one shown at the right, you see that both left and right arrows are showing yellow. You should expect that shortly the right arrow light will go

22.____

    A.   red, and the left arrow light will go green
    B.   green, and the left arrow light will go red
    C.   red, and the left arrow light will go red
    D.   green, and the left arrow light will go green

23. With an automatic transmission, it is NOT desirable to shift from the "Drive" to the "Intermediate" or "Low" position when driving down a steep hill because

23.____

    A.   there will be no increase in the braking power of the engine
    B.   the gears will not engage while the car is in motion
    C.   the low speed gears may engage with the low speed gears and wreck the transmission
    D.   the car may skid if the road is slippery

24. When entering a two-way street from a private garage driveway, you

24.____

    A.   do not have the right of way over traffic approaching from the right but only over traffic approaching from the left
    B.   have the right of way over traffic approaching only from the right
    C.   have the right of way over traffic approaching from both right and left
    D.   do not have the right of way over traffic approaching from either right or left

25. In the state, a report need not be made to the Department of Motor Vehicles of any motor vehicle accident in which there is

25.____

    A.   personal injury only
    B.   personal injury and property damage of less than $100
    C.   property damage of more than $100 but no personal injury
    D.   injury to a horse or a dog

26. When the level of the liquid in a battery gets too low, it is necessary to put in some more

26.____

    A.   battery acid   B.   hydroxide
    C.   distilled water   D.   tap water

27. When the temperature indicator shows the engine running cold, even after the car has been driven for about ten minutes, the trouble is USUALLY caused by

27.____

    A.   a broken fan belt
    B.   a thermostat out of order
    C.   a frozen radiator
    D.   too little liquid in the cooling system

28. If you had to choose the oil for the crankcase of a new model passenger car motor, it would be SAFEST to use

28.____

    A.   machine oil   B.   transmission oil
    C.   S.A.E. 20-20W oil   D.   S.A.E. 50 oil

29. Inspection of your car's front tires shows that the tread is greatly worn on both the outer and inner edges of both tires. This is USUALLY a sign of   29._____

    A. underinflation   B. overinflation
    C. misalignment   D. unbalance

30. In washing the outside of a dirty car, the MOST effective cleanser is   30._____

    A. gasoline
    B. soap and water
    C. a detergent cleanser and water
    D. benzine

31. The MOST probable cause of a complete loss of oil pressure while driving is   31._____

    A. a crankcase oil level which is too low
    B. a crankcase oil level which is too high
    C. the use of too thick an oil
    D. an obstruction in the oil line

32. Proper tire inflation pressures are measured BEST by the   32._____

    A. eye; the tire should have the same shape on bottom as on top
    B. tire wear; the tire should wear evenly
    C. use of a tire gage
    D. hardness of the tire

33. In order to change a tire MOST safely and effectively, it is sufficient to have a   33._____

    A. jack, lug wrench, screwdriver, and wheel blocks
    B. screwdriver, lug wrench, and jack
    C. jack, screwdriver, hammer, and tire gage
    D. screwdriver, wheel blocks, and jack

34. While traveling on a two-way roadway having two traffic lanes in each direction and hearing the siren and seeing the flashing red light of a fire truck approaching from the rear, the driver of a motor vehicle should   34._____

    A. stop immediately
    B. pull over to the right-hand side of the roadway and proceed slowly in order not to block traffic
    C. pull over into the nearest intersection and stop
    D. pull over to the right-hand side of the roadway and stop

35. For the sole purpose of discharging a passenger, it is illegal to stop a motor vehicle   35._____

    A. within 10 feet of a fire hydrant during daylight hours
    B. in a marked bus stop when no bus is in sight
    C. in a zone marked "No Standing"
    D. in a zone marked "No Stopping"

36. The Vehicle and Traffic Law states that every motor vehicle must have its headlamps lit   36.____
    when being driven upon a public highway between

    A. dusk and dawn
    B. sunset and sunrise
    C. one-half hour before sunset and one-half hour after sunrise
    D. one-half hour after sunset and one-half hour before sunrise

37. With regard to "Stop" signs at intersections, which of the following statements is COR-   37.____
    RECT?

    A. A motorist approaching a "Stop" sign need not come to a complete stop, but he
       must slow down before driving through the intersection or he loses the right of way.
    B. At an intersection with a "Stop" sign, a police officer directing traffic can wave on a
       motorist to permit him to pass through the intersection without stopping.
    C. At an intersection with a "Stop" sign, a motorist must stop no matter what the police
       officer who is directing traffic there signals him to do.
    D. After stopping for a "Stop" sign at an intersection, the driver of the stopped car has
       the right of way over all cars in, or approaching, the intersection.

38. You are driving straight ahead on a state highway marked with a double solid line down   38.____
    the middle (═══════════) .
    You may

    A. nor cross this line
    B. cross from either side if there is no oncoming traffic
    C. cross only from right to left
    D. cross only from left to right

39. You are driving straight ahead on a state highway marked with a solid and broken double   39.____
    line down the middle (═══════════) .
    You may

    A. not cross the line from either side
    B. cross the line from either side at any time with caution
    C. cross the line from the broken line side only
    D. cross the line from the solid line side only with extreme caution if traffic permits

40. It is LEAST correct to say that a broken line (----------) painted along the length of   40.____
    a state highway

    A. defines traffic lanes
    B. may not be crossed at any time
    C. may be crossed from either side
    D. may be crossed only if crossing will not interfere with traffic

41. When traveling at 30 miles per hour, a car with four wheel brakes MUST be able to stop   41.____
    within _____ feet.

    A. 45   B. 180   C. 67   D. 100

42. Square road traffic signs mean   42.____

    A. caution   B. stop
    C. reduce speed   D. danger

43. Statistics show that drivers under 20 years of age have a higher accident rate than other   43.____
age groups. This is probably due to the fact that

    A. younger drivers are not as quick-witted as older ones
    B. it takes about seven years to develop good driving ability
    C. youthful drivers are inclined to take more chances
    D. most drivers are under 20 years of age

44. The MOST serious type of accident is caused by   44.____

    A. a rear-end collision
    B. a moving vehicle hitting a parked car
    C. the blowout of a tire
    D. a head-on collision

45. License plates MUST be fastened to a motor vehicle   45.____

    A. at least 12 inches from the top of the vehicle
    B. about 48 inches from the ground
    C. between 12 and 48 inches from the ground
    D. so as to be visible at 350 feet

46. The one of the following which may NOT be crossed at any time is a   46.____

    A. single solid line   B. broken line
    C. solid and broken line   D. double solid line

47. A "defensive driver" is one who   47.____

    A. makes allowances for the weaknesses of other drivers
    B. is always apologizing for his poor driving
    C. blames the other driver when he is involved in an accident
    D. drives very slowly at the extreme right side of the road

48. The height of a vehicle from the under side of the tire to the top of the vehicle, including   48.____
load, may NOT be more than _____ feet.

    A. 15   B. 10   C. 8   D. 13

49. The one of the following which is NOT classed as a crime is   49.____

    A. parking overtime
    B. operating an unregistered motor vehicle
    C. driving without a license
    D. removing a serial number on an automobile engine

50. When a car starts to skid,

   A. the brakes should be applied forcefully
   B. the wheels should be turned in the opposite direction
   C. accelerate gently
   D. put the gears in neutral

50._____

KEY (CORRECT ANSWERS)

1.	A	11.	C	21.	B	31.	A	41.	C
2.	C	12.	D	22.	C	32.	C	42.	A
3.	D	13.	D	23.	D	33.	A	43.	C
4.	A	14.	C	24.	D	34.	D	44.	D
5.	D	15.	D	25.	D	35.	D	45.	C
6.	B	16.	D	26.	C	36.	D	46.	D
7.	D	17.	A	27.	B	37.	B	47.	A
8.	D	18.	D	28.	C	38.	A	48.	D
9.	B	19.	A	29.	A	39.	C	49.	A
10.	A	20.	B	30.	C	40.	B	50.	C

TEST 2

DIRECTIONS: Each question or incomplete statement is followed by several suggested answers or completions. Select the one that BEST answers the question or completes the statement. *PRINT THE LETTER OF THE CORRECT ANSWER IN THE SPACE AT THE RIGHT.*

1. Garage floors are to be kept free of oil and grease. The MAIN reason for such a rule is that oil and grease spots on a garage floor

    A. are breeding places for germs
    B. develop an unpleasant odor
    C. increase the chance of accidents
    D. show poor maintenance of vehicles

1.____

2. After you return from lunch, you find that the new city car, which you parked at the curb, has a big scratch on the right front door. There is no one around.
The BEST thing for you to do is to

    A. get the license number of the vehicle that did the damage
    B. lay out some money for touch-up enamel and make the repair
    C. question passersby to find someone who will be willing to be a witness for the city
    D. report the damage to the garage foreman when you get back to the garage

2.____

3. Suppose that the dispatcher has assigned you to drive a diesel truck during the regular operator's vacation. You have never operated this type of vehicle.
For you to tell this to the dispatcher would be

    A. foolish, because the dispatcher will think you do not want to cooperate
    B. sensible, because an inexperienced operator may damage the equipment
    C. foolish, because this is a good chance to learn how to operate a diesel truck
    D. sensible, because your regular assignment is an easier job than operation of the truck

3.____

4. A motor vehicle operator is assigned to drive another city employee who is delivering several bulky packages to a city building. Upon arrival at the building, it would be MOST desirable for the motor vehicle operator to

    A. ask the other employee if he can give him any help in carrying the packages into the building
    B. leave for the garage as soon as the packages have been unloaded onto the side-walk
    C. load the packages onto the employee's arms and go with him into the building in case he should need any assistance
    D. wait inside the vehicle for a few minutes and then leave

4.____

5. When the light at an intersection changes from red to green, the driver of the car nearest the corner does not go ahead because he is waiting for pedestrians to clear the cross-walk.
If the driver of the car behind starts to blow his horn, the driver of the first car should

    A. call a policeman to give the horn-blower a ticket for making unnecessary noise
    B. get out of his vehicle so that he can explain why he could not go ahead

5.____

    C.   pay no attention to the horn-blower and go ahead after the pedestrians are out of the way

    D.   lean out the window and shout angrily to the driver behind to stop blowing his horn

6.   When he returns to the garage after driving several passengers during the day, a motor vehicle operator finds a set of keys on the floor of his vehicle.
    The BEST thing for the operator to do is to   6.____

    A.   keep the keys in case he sees any of these passengers again
    B.   take the keys to the police department's lost property unit
    C.   telephone each passenger to find out who lost the keys
    D.   turn the keys over to his supervisor

7.   The garage foreman has asked the motor vehicle operators in your garage to try out a new system for making out daily mileage reports.
    Suppose that you do not think the new system is necessary. You should   7.____

    A.   continue to use the old system to make out your daily mileage reports
    B.   make out no reports until after the foreman decides on a final system
    C.   use the new system even though you think the change is not necessary
    D.   write a complaint to the foreman's supervisor that the new system is unnecessary

8.   Recently, the city has been carrying on an anti-jaywalking drive for pedestrians.
    The success of this drive is important to motorists MAINLY because   8.____

    A.   the pedestrian will then be just as much at fault as the driver if there is an accident
    B.   there will be less chance of a vehicle hitting a pedestrian
    C.   traffic will move more quickly
    D.   vehicles will then have the right of way

9.   After you have driven a city official to an office building, he asks you to wait in the parked car saying that he will be out in fifteen minutes.
    When, after twenty-five minutes, he still hasn't come out, it would be BEST for you to   9.____

    A.   call the garage and ask what to do
    B.   continue to wait in the car until he comes out
    C.   enter the building to find the official and tell him that fifteen minutes are past and he may be late for other appointments
    D.   go for a cup of coffee since he seems to be delayed, but come right back

10.   A motor vehicle operator who does NOT clearly understand the dispatcher's route instruction should first   10.____

    A.   ask an experienced motor vehicle operator the best route to follow
    B.   ask the American Automobile Association to recommend a route
    C.   ask the dispatcher to explain the route more fully
    D.   figure out his own route using an official map

Questions 11-13.

DIRECTIONS: Answer Questions 11 to 13 ONLY on the basis of the information given in the following paragraph.

A National Safety Council study of 685,000 traffic accidents reveals that most accidents happen under "safe" conditions - in clear, dry weather, on straight roads, and when traffic volumes are low. The point is, most accidents can be attributed to lapses on the part of the drivers rather than traffic or road conditions or deliberate law violations. Most drivers try to avoid accidents. Why, then, do so many get into trouble? A major cause is the average motorist's failure to recognize a hazard soon enough to avoid it entirely. He does not, by habit, notice the clues that are there for him to see. He takes constant risks in traffic without even knowing it. These faulty seeing habits plus the common distractions that all drivers must deal with, such as hurry, worry, daydreaming, impatience, concentration on route problems, add up to a guaranteed answer - an accident.

11. According to a study by the National Safety Council, MOST accidents can be blamed on   11._____

    A. curving, hilly roads
    B. errors made by drivers
    C. heavy streams of traffic
    D. wet, foggy weather

12. According to the above paragraph, an IMPORTANT reason why the average motorist   12._____
gets into an accident is that he

    A. does not see the danger of an accident soon enough
    B. does not try to avoid accidents
    C. drives at too great a speed
    D. purposely takes reckless chances

13. According to the above paragraph, it is NOT reasonable to say that drivers are distracted   13._____
from their driving and possibly involved in an accident because they

    A. are impatient about something
    B. concentrate on the road ahead
    C. hurry to get to where they are going
    D. worry about some problem

Questions 14-17.

DIRECTIONS: Answer Questions 14 to 17 ONLY on the basis of the information given in the following paragraph.

If a good automobile map is studied thoroughly before a trip is started, much useful information can be learned. This information may help to decrease the cost of and the time required for the trip and, at the same time, increase the safety and comfort of the trip. The legend found on the face of the map explains symbols and markings and the kind of roads on various routes. The legend also explains how to tell by width, color, or type of line whether the road is dual- or multiple-lane, and whether it is paved, all-weather, graded, earth, under construction, or proposed for construction. Federal routes are usually shown by a number within a shield and state routes by a number within a circle. The legend also shows scale of miles on a bar marked to indicate the distance each portion of the bar represents on the earth's surface. Distances between locations on the map are shown by plain numerals beside the route lines; they indicate mileage between marked points or intersections. Add the mileage numbers shown along a route to determine distances.

14. According to the above paragraph, the markings on the road map will show   14.____

     A.   a different color for a road proposed for construction than for one under construction
     B.   a double line if a road is a dual-lane road
     C.   what part of a road is damaged or being repaired
     D.   which roads on state routes have more than two lanes

15. The above paragraph does NOT mention as a possible advantage of studying a good   15.____
road map before beginning a trip the

     A.   increase in interest of the trip
     B.   reduction in the chance of an accident on the trip
     C.   saving of money
     D.   saving of time

16. According to the above paragraph, in order to find the total mileage of a certain route, a   16.____
motorist should add the numbers

     A.   on the bar scale in the legend
     B.   between marked points beside the route lines
     C.   inside a shield along the route
     D.   within a circle along the route

17. According to the above paragraph, the legend on a road map includes information which   17.____
a motorist could use to

     A.   choose the best paved route
     B.   figure the toll charges
     C.   find the allowable speed limits
     D.   learn the location of bridges

Questions 18-22.

DIRECTIONS: The following report is similar to those used in departments for reporting accidents. Read it carefully, then answer Questions 18 to 22 using ONLY the information given in the report.

REPORT OF ACCIDENT

Date of Report: 3/24
Time: 3:43 P.M.

Date of Accident: 3/21
<u>Department Vehicle</u>   <u>Vehicle No. 2</u>

Operator's Name: James Doe   Operator's Name: Richard Roe
Title: Motor Vehicle Operator   Operator's Address: 841 W. 68th St.
Vehicle Code No.: 22-187   Owner's Name: Jane Roe
License Plate No.: 3N-1234   Owner's Address: 2792 Beal Ave.
                                      License Plate No.: 8Y-6789

Damage to Vehicle: right rear   Damage to Vehicle: grill, radiator
fender ripped, hubcap dented,   right side of front bumper,
rear bumper twisted.   front fender and headlight crushed.
Place of Accident: 8th Ave. &
48th Street

Description of Accident: I was driving east on 48th Street with the green light. I was almost across 8th Avenue when Ford panel truck started north and crashed into my rear right fender. Driver of Ford used abussive language and accused me of rolling into his truck.

Persons Injured

Name Richard Roe   Address   841 W. 68th Street

Name   Address

Name   Address

Witnesses

Name Richard Roe   Address   841 W. 68th Street

Name John Brown   Address   226 South Avenue

Name Mary Green   Address   42 East Street

Report Prepared by   James Doe

Title MVO   Badge No.   11346

18. Of the following words used in the report, the one spelled INCORRECTLY is   18.____

   A. abussive   B. accused   C. radiator   D. twisted

19. The city vehicle involved in this accident can BEST be identified   19.____

   A. as a panel truck
   B. as a passenger car
   C. by the badge number of the operator
   D. by the vehicle code number

20. According to the information in the report, the right of way belonged to   20.____

   A. neither vehicle   B. the Department vehicle
   C. the vehicle that took it   D. vehicle No. 2

21. An entry on the report that seems to be INCORRECT is the   21.____

   A. first witness   B. second witness
   C. third witness   D. owner's name

22. According to the description of the accident, the diagram that would BEST show how and   22.____
where the vehicles crashed is:

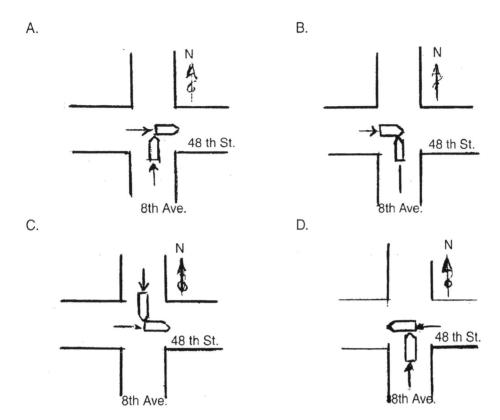

A.

B.

C.

D.

Questions 23-24.

DIRECTIONS: Answer Questions 23 and 24 ONLY on the basis of the information given in the following paragraph.

When heavy rain beats on your windshield, it becomes hard for you to see ahead and even harder to see objects to the side - despite good windshield wipers. Also, the danger zone 'becomes longer when it is raining because the car takes longer to stop on wet streets. Remember that the danger zone of your car is the distance within which you can't stop after you have seen something on the road ahead of your car. The way to reduce the length of the danger zone of your car while driving is to reduce speed.

23.   From the information in the above paragraph, you cannot tell if the danger zone of your car

    23.____

    A.   can be made smaller
    B.   is greater on a rainy day
    C.   is greater on cloudy days than on clear days
    D.   is the distance in back of the car or in front of the car

24.   According to the above paragraph, the danger zone of a moving car is affected by

    24.____

    A.   the condition of the street and the speed of the car
    B.   many things which cannot be pinned down, in addition to the mechanical condition of the car
    C.   the number of objects to the front and to the side
    D.   visibility of the road and the reaction time of the driver

25. In the city it is not permissible for the operator to drive in any direction on a one-way   25.____
street if he is operating a

    A. fire department vehicle in response to an alarm
    B. police department vehicle in response to a radio call
    C. hospital department ambulance in response to a call on that street
    D. United States mail truck while collecting mail

26. In the city, a flashing yellow light at an intersection indicates that the driver should   26.____

    A. blow his horn before making a left or right turn
    B. come to a full stop, then proceed with caution
    C. not make any turns but may proceed directly ahead
    D. proceed through the intersection with caution

27. A driver of a passenger vehicle would be guilty of a violation of city traffic regulations if he   27.____

    A. parked his car in an area marked "1 Hour Parking" and proceeded to wash the car
    B. remained in the driver's seat while the car stood alongside a fire hydrant during the
daytime
    C. stopped in an area marked "Taxi Stand" to discharge a passenger
    D. stopped to pick up a passenger in an area marked "No Standing"

28. According to the State Vehicle and Traffic Law, when there is a motor accident in which a   28.____
person is injured, an accident report MUST be filed with the Bureau of Motor Vehicles by

    A. both the driver and owner of the car responsible for the accident
    B. each driver separately if more than one car was involved
    C. the driver of only the car responsible for the accident
    D. the injured person or his representative

29. In the city, a driver is allowed to park in a metered area without putting a coin in the park-   29.____
ing meter if the

    A. car being parked is a city vehicle
    B. driver stays in the car
    C. meter is covered with a bag marked "out of order"
    D. meter shows there is still unused time on it

30. A traffic sign cannot be read because the printing on it is covered with snow. A motor   30.____
vehicle operator should bring his vehicle to a full stop when he reaches this sign if it is
shaped like

    A. △   B. ▢   C. ◇   D. ⬡

Questions 31-34.

DIRECTIONS: Questions 31 to 34 are diagrams of road markings used in the state. From Column I, select the traffic rule that applies to each road marking. Indicate your answer in the space at the right.

<u>COLUMN I</u>

31.

A.   crossing allowed from either dotted line side

31.____

B.   crossing allowed from either side at any time

32.

C.   crossing allowed from either side at any time

32.____

D.   line may be crossed cautiously except in the city

33.

E.   no crossing allowed from either side at any time

33.____

34.

34.____

35.   Keeping the gas tank of a car well-filled is a good practice MAINLY because it helps   35.____

   A.   add weight to the car, resulting in smoother riding
   B.   avoid frequent stops for gasoline
   C.   prevent watering of the gasoline due to excess condensation of moisture
   D.   the operator to keep a close check on gas consumption of the vehicle

36.   The odometer is the instrument on a motor vehicle which indicates the   36.____

   A.   amount of electric current flowing to or from the battery
   B.   number of miles the car has traveled
   C.   oil pressure needed to pump lubricating oil to the engine
   D.   speed, in miles per hour, at which the car is traveling

37.   You can think of a car as made of two major units: A -the engine; B - the body and chassis. The one of the following which is used to disconnect the power of A from B while keeping the car in gear is the   37.____

   A.   clutch   B.   differential
   C.   transmission   D.   universal

38. Of the following, the MAIN purpose of the fan connected to the automobile engine is to cool the

    38.____

    A. air as it goes into the engine
    B. engine oil as it goes through the oil filter
    C. exhaust manifold
    D. water in the radiator

Questions 39-48.

DIRECTIONS: Answers to Questions 39 to 48, inclusive, are based on the map appearing on Page 10.

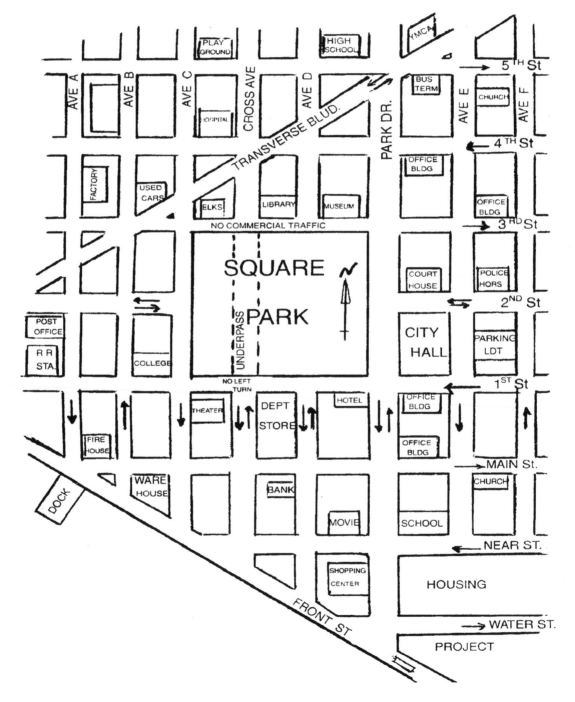

39. To drive from the courthouse to the railroad station, the MOST direct allowable route is   39.____

    A. across 2nd Street, Avenue A, 1st Street
    B. through the underpass in Square Park
    C. 2nd Street, Park Drive, and 1st Street
    D. 2nd Street, Park Drive, and 3rd Street

40. A left turn is prohibited at   40.____

    A. 1st Street and Cross Avenue
    B. 1st Street and Park Drive
    C. Avenue C and 2nd Street
    D. 4th Street and Transverse Boulevard

41. The direction of traffic on Front Street is   41.____

    A. east and west
    B. northwest and southeast
    C. southwest and northeast
    D. the same as on Transverse Boulevard

42. When driving from the Y.M.C.A. to the dock by the SHORTEST allowable route, the   42.____
direction of travel would be, in order,

    A. east, south, west   B. southwest, west, south
    C. southwest, south   D. west, south

43. When driving from the post office to the movie by the SHORTEST allowable route, the   43.____
direction of travel would be, in order,

    A. north, east, south, east
    B. south, east, south, west
    C. south, southeast, north, east
    D. south, southeast, east

44. The two buildings which face on both Cross Avenue and Avenue D are the   44.____

    A. bank and the department store
    B. department store and the hotel
    C. department store and the library
    D. library and the museum

45. The MOST direct allowable route that a truck may take from the factory to the bus termi-   45.____
nal is Avenue A and

    A. 2nd Street, Avenue B, 5th Street
    B. 3rd Street, Transverse Boulevard, 5th Street
    C. 5th Street
    D. Transverse Boulevard, 5th Street, 2nd Street

46. The SHORTEST allowable route from the office building on 1st Street to the parking lot is   46.____
    1st Street,

    A.   Avenue E
    B.   Avenue F
    C.   Park Drive, 2nd Street, Avenue E
    D.   Park Drive, Main Street, Avenue F

47. In driving from the museum to the theatre, the MOST direct route allowable for a passen-   47.____
    ger car is 3rd Street,

    A.   Avenue C
    B.   Park Drive, 1st Street, Avenue C
    C.   Park Drive, 1st Street, Cross Avenue
    D.   Square Park underpass, 1st Street, Avenue C

48. The shopping center is on a street where traffic is   48.____

    A.   one way, north
    B.   one way, south
    C.   two ways, east and west
    D.   two ways, north and south

49. Of the following, the MAIN disadvantage of using alcohol as an anti-freeze in the cooling   49.____
    system of a motor vehicle is that alcohol

    A.   is poisonous and cannot be handled safely
    B.   is thin and finds holes in the cooling system
    C.   boils and evaporates at an undesirably high temperature
    D.   boils and evaporates at an undesirably low temperature

50. To keep the clutch pedal fully down while starting the engine of a gearshift car is   50.____

    A.   *bad* practice because it wears out the clutch
    B.   *good* practice because it reduces the work required of the starter
    C.   *bad* practice because it will cause the car to jerk forward if it is in gear
    D.   *good* practice because it saves fuel

KEY (CORRECT ANSWERS)

1. C	11. B	21. A	31. C	41. B
2. D	12. A	22. A	32. E	42. C
3. B	13. B	23. C	33. A	43. B
4. A	14. D	24. A	34. D	44. C
5. C	15. A	25. D	35. C	45. B
6. D	16. B	26. D	36. B	46. C
7. C	17. A	27. A	37. A	47. B
8. B	18. A	28. B	38. D	48. D
9. B	19. D	29. D	39. C	49. D
10. C	20. B	30. D	40. A	50. B

EXAMINATION SECTION
TEST 1

DIRECTIONS: Each question or incomplete statement is followed by several suggested answers or completions. Select the one that BEST answers the question or completes the statement. *PRINT THE LETTER OF THE CORRECT ANSWER IN THE SPACE AT THE RIGHT.*

1. Your car's brakes transform one type of energy into another.
   Which of the following BEST describes the change?

   A. Kinetic energy into heat
   B. Centrifugal force into force of impact
   C. Gravity into kinetic energy
   D. Centrifugal force into heat

   1.____

2. Which of the following qualities is MOST important in driving a motor vehicle?

   A. Fast reaction time   B. Courage
   C. Skill   D. Judgment

   2.____

3. Glaring headlights add to night driving hazards. Which of the following should you NOT do?

   A. Lower your headlight beams in advance of meeting other cars
   B. Reduce your speed when facing headlight glare
   C. Focus your eyes downward on the center line of the road instead of up into the oncoming lights
   D. Lower your headlight beams when following another car

   3.____

4. The following institutions lend money for the purchase of cars.
   Which charges the LOWEST rate of interest?

   A. Banks
   B. Pawnshops
   C. Installment finance companies
   D. Personal loan companies

   4.____

5. Under what conditions do we find the GREATEST traction?

   A. Wet concrete pavement
   B. Dry concrete pavement
   C. Dry concrete pavement with sand on it
   D. Bumpy, uneven pavement

   5.____

6. Your danger zone is

   A. the longest distance at which you can see and recognize danger
   B. your stopping distance
   C. the distance at which a vehicle in back of your car is following
   D. your braking distance

   6.____

7. For sound financing of a purchase of an automobile, you would have to raise a down payment of AT LEAST _____ of the value of the car.

    A. 10 percent   B. 25 percent
    C. one-third   D. one-half

7.____

8. Which of the following is characteristic of older paved roads and not of modern highways?

    A. Median strips   B. High road crowns
    C. Road banking   D. Long sight distances

8.____

9. Designed especially for slowing down to prepare to leave the freeway is the

    A. deceleration lane   B. median strip
    C. ramp   D. road shoulder

9.____

10. When you find yourself getting very sleepy while driving on a long trip, the BEST remedy is

    A. black coffee   B. fresh air
    C. Benzedrine   D. sleep

10.____

11. Which of these four types of insurance does a bank or other lender require the purchaser to have?

    A. Collision   B. Comprehensive
    C. Liability   D. Medical payment

11.____

12. The professional specialist who plans the operation of highways is the

    A. Commissioner of Motor Vehicles
    B. highway engineer
    C. traffic engineer
    D. Commissioner of State Police

12.____

13. Which of the following is the CORRECT formula?

    A. Braking distance + stopping distance = reaction distance
    B. Reaction distance + stopping distance = braking distance
    C. Reaction distance + braking distance = stopping distance
    D. Reaction distance + danger zone = stopping distance

13.____

14. Which of the following is a YIELD sign?

    A.   B.   C.   D.

14.____

15. When you drive around a curve, which of the following helps you to do it safely?

    A. Centrifugal force   B. Friction
    C. Kinetic energy   D. Force of impact

15.____

16. If you are involved in an accident, which of the following things should you NOT do?   16._____

    A. Show your driver's license and vehicle registration card and make note of the information on those of the driver of the other car.
    B. If any person seems to be seriously injured, place him in your car immediately and proceed at once to the nearest hospital.
    C. Submit accident reports as indicated by your state and local regulations.
    D. Notify your insurance company.

17. No person should drive in dense fog unless it is absolutely necessary.   17._____
When it does prove necessary, he should use

    A. parking lights
    B. high-beam headlights
    C. low-beam headlights
    D. no lights, to avoid distortion of vision

18. Under which of the following would you classify the wearing of glasses to aid vision?   18._____

    A. Compensation   B. Field of vision
    C. Correction   D. Adjustment

19. The key words for driving on a slippery surface are   19._____

    A. firmly and accurately   B. gently and gradually
    C. strongly and steadily   D. quickly and surely

20. Which of the following types of insurance is MOST important to a car owner?   20._____

    A. Collision   B. Liability
    C. Comprehensive   D. Medical payment

KEY (CORRECT ANSWERS)

1.	C	11.	A
2.	D	12.	C
3.	D	13.	C
4.	A	14.	D
5.	B	15.	A
6.	B	16.	B
7.	C	17.	C
8.	B	18.	C
9.	A	19.	B
10.	D	20.	B

TEST 2

DIRECTIONS: Each question or incomplete statement is followed by several suggested answers or completions. Select the one that BEST answers the question or completes the statement. *PRINT THE LETTER OF THE CORRECT ANSWER IN THE SPACE AT THE RIGHT.*

1. Which of these four items is a *grade separation?*   1.____

   A. A divided highway
   B. A change in the slope of a hill
   C. Bushes planted between two roadways on which traffic moves in opposite directions
   D. A cloverleaf

2. Which of the following blood alcohol concentrations should be used to establish that a driver is *under the influence of alcohol?*   2.____

   A. 0.05%   B. 0.10%   C. 0.15%   D. 0.6%

3. Three of the following four statements are true of freeways. Which statement is NOT true?   3.____

   A. They have a limited number of interchanges at which vehicles may enter or leave the freeway.
   B. They have a limited number of STOP and GO signals.
   C. Traffic moving in opposite directions is not separated by a median strip.
   D. Crossing the median strip is not permitted.

4. To correct a skid, you should   4.____

   A. steer in the direction in which the rear of the car is skidding
   B. steer in the direction opposite that in which the rear of the car is skidding
   C. hold the steering wheel firmly in the straight-ahead position
   D. use the parking or handbrake so that only the rear wheels will lock while the front wheels turn freely

5. The MOST dangerous effects of alcohol on the driver are those concerned with   5.____

   A. vision
   B. reaction time
   C. behavior
   D. coordination and driving skill

6. The *Three E's* of traffic safety are included in the following four words. Which of them is NOT one of the *Three E's?*   6.____

   A. Education   B. Engineering
   C. Enforcement   D. Efficiency

7. Which of the following BEST describes the true meaning of the word *courage?*   7.____

   A. Ability to overcome fear
   B. Absence of fear
   C. Taking chances to gain a reputation as a daredevil
   D. Lack of realization of the true nature of danger

8. Which of the following types of insurance is of GREATEST importance to you when you own a car?   8.____

    A. Liability
    B. Collision
    C. Comprehensive
    D. Medical payment

9. Which of the following statements is NOT correct?   9.____

    A. Most states have legalized the use of electric directional signals to signal turns.
    B. Overheating is always due to failures in the cooling system.
    C. Power brakes do not decrease the stopping distance.
    D. The horn should never be sounded except in the interest of safety.

10. Three of the following are good safety features. Which is NOT a safety feature?   10.____

    A. Door locks
    B. Rear-view mirror inside the car
    C. Eye-level outside mirror
    D. Ventilation of the inside of the car

11. The MOST important factor in good car maintenance is   11.____

    A. an honest, dependable service station or garage
    B. a skilled mechanic
    C. high quality, reliable parts
    D. a responsible car owner

12. Three of the following procedures will add to tire traction in starting your car on ice. Which one will NOT help?   12.____

    A. Letting some air out of the rear tires
    B. Sprinkling sand on the ice
    C. Slipping the clutch
    D. Feeding gas more gently and more gradually

13. The four-stroke cycle includes THREE of the following. Which of the following is NOT part of the cycle? _____ stroke.   13.____

    A. Intake
    B. Compression
    C. Power
    D. Completion

14. Vehicles A, C, and D in the illustration shown at the right have stopped to allow vehicle B to turn.
Which vehicle, A, C, or D, would be the FIRST to cross the intersection, considering right-of-way rules?   14.____

    A. A
    B. C
    C. D
    D. None of the above

15. What part of the cost of planning, designing, and constructing the National System of   15.____
    Interstate and Defense Highways is paid for by Federal-aid funds?

    A. 90%   B. 50%   C. 10%   D. 100%

16. When you leave a freeway and drive on a city street, you must check your speed fre-   16.____
    quently because you may be

    A. accelerated
    B. suffering from highway hypnosis
    C. velocitized
    D. suffering impairment of vision due to carbon monoxide

17. Which of the following statements is CORRECT?   17.____

    A. Certain drugs, like Benzedrine in *keep-awake* pills, actually make driving at night
        safe.
    B. A driver should trust no one but a physician to determine whether or not he should
        drive after taking any kind of drug.
    C. The Federal Food and Drug Act does not permit the sale of any drug dangerous to
        a driver without a prescription from a registered physician.
    D. The individual driver must rely entirely upon his judgment and knowledge of how a
        specific drug will affect him.

18. Three of the following four maintenance procedures are good.   18.____
    Which is NOT a good procedure?

    A. Rotate your tires to avoid uneven wear.
    B. Avoid letting oil or gasoline come into contact with your tires.
    C. For driving in very hot weather, underinflate your tires to avoid building up exces-
        sive pressure in them.
    D. Keep the battery terminals covered with a light layer of grease.

19. Drivers should be able to recognize traffic signs by their shape.   19.____
    Which of the following signs warns drivers that they are approaching a railroad grade
    crossing?

    A.   B.   C.   D.

20. Imagine that the steering wheel is the face of a clock.   20.____
    The driver's hands should grasp it at _____ and _____ o'clock.

    A. 8; 4   B. 9; 3   C. 10; 2   D. 11; 1

KEY (CORRECT ANSWERS)

1.	D	11.	C
2.	A	12.	A
3.	B	13.	D
4.	A	14.	C
5.	D	15.	A
6.	C	16.	C
7.	A	17.	B
8.	A	18.	C
9.	B	19.	B
10.	C	20.	C

MAP READING

EXAMINATION SECTION
TEST 1

DIRECTIONS: Each question or incomplete statement is followed by several suggested answers or completions. Select the one that BEST answers the question or completes the statement. *PRINT THE LETTER OF THE CORRECT ANSWER IN THE SPACE AT THE RIGHT.* ̄

Questions 1-3.

DIRECTIONS: Questions 1 through 3 are to be answered SOLELY on the basis of the map which appears on the next page. The flow of traffic is indicated by the arrow. If there is only one arrow shown, then traffic flows only in the direction indicated by the arrow. If there are two arrows shown, then traffic flows in both directions. You must follow the flow of traffic.

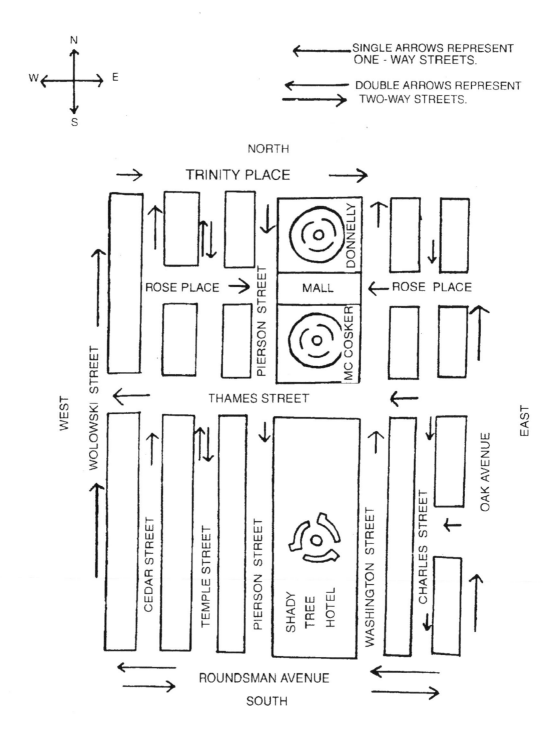

SINGLE ARROWS REPRESENT ONE - WAY STREETS.

DOUBLE ARROWS REPRESENT TWO-WAY STREETS.

1. Police Officers Simms and O'Brien are located at Roundsman Avenue and Washington   1._____
    Street. The radio dispatcher has assigned them to investigate a motor vehicle accident at
    the corner of Pierson Street and Rose Place.
    Which one of the following is the SHORTEST route for them to take in their patrol car,
    making sure to obey all traffic regulations?
    Travel

    A. west on Roundsman Avenue, then north on Temple Street, then east on Thames
        Street, then north on Pierson Street to Rose Place
    B. east on Roundsman Avenue, then north on Oak Avenue, then west on Rose Place
        to Pierson Street
    C. west on Roundsman Avenue, then north on Temple Street, then east on Rose
        Place to Pierson Street
    D. east on Roundsman Avenue, then north on Oak Avenue, then west on Thames
        Street, then north on Temple Street, then east on Rose Place to Pierson Street

2. Police Officers Sears and Castro are located at Cedar Street and Roundsman Avenue.   2._____
    They are called to respond to the scene of a burglary at Rose Place and Charles Street.
    Which one of the following is the SHORTEST route for them to take in their patrol car,
    making sure to obey all traffic regulations?
    Travel

    A. east on Roundsman Avenue, then north on Oak Avenue, then west on Rose Place
        to Charles Street
    B. east on Roundsman Avenue, then north on Washington Street, then east on Rose
        Place to Charles Street
    C. west on Roundsman Avenue, then north on Wolowski Street, then east on Trinity
        Place, then south on Charles Street to Rose Place
    D. east on Roundsman Avenue, then north on Charles Street to Rose Place

3. Police Officer Glasser is in an unmarked car at the intersection of Rose Place and Tem-   3._____
    ple Street when he begins to follow two robbery suspects. The suspects go south for two
    blocks, then turn left for two blocks, then make another left turn for one more block. The
    suspects realize they are being followed and make a left turn and travel two more blocks
    and then make a right turn.
    In what direction are the suspects now headed?

    A. North   B. South   C. East   D. West

Questions 4-6.

DIRECTIONS: Questions 4 through 6 are to be answered SOLELY on the basis of the follow-
             ing map. The flow of traffic is indicated by the arrows. If there is only one arrow
             shown, then traffic flows only in the direction indicated by the arrow. If there are
             two arrows shown, then traffic flows in both directions. You must follow the flow
             of traffic.

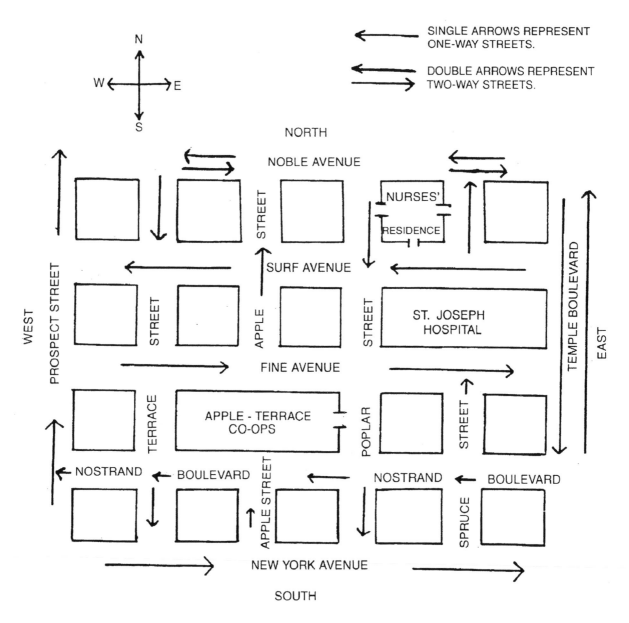

4. Police Officers Gannon and Vine are located at the intersection of Terrace Street and   4._____
   Surf Avenue when they receive a call from the radio dispatcher stating that they need to
   respond to an attempted murder at Spruce Street and Fine Avenue.
   Which one of the following is the SHORTEST route for them to take in their patrol car,
   making sure to obey all traffic regulations?
   Travel _____ to Spruce Street.

   A.   west on Surf Avenue, then north on Prospect Street, then east on Noble Avenue,
        then south on Poplar Street, then east on Fine Avenue
   B.   east on Surf Avenue, then south on Poplar Street, then east on Fine Avenue
   C.   west on Surf Avenue, then south on Prospect Street, then east on Fine Avenue
   D.   south on Terrace Street, then east on Fine Avenue

5. Police Officers Sears and Ronald are at Nostrand Boulevard and Prospect Street. They receive a call assigning them to investigate a disruptive group of youths at Temple Boulevard and Surf Avenue.
Which one of the following is the SHORTEST route for them to take in their patrol car, making sure to obey all traffic regulations?
Travel

    A.   north on Prospect Street, then east on Surf Avenue to Temple Boulevard
    B.   north on Prospect Street, then east on Noble Avenue, then south on Temple Boulevard to Surf Avenue
    C.   north on Prospect Street, then east on Fine Avenue, then north on Temple Boulevard to Surf Avenue
    D.   south on Prospect Street, then east on New York Avenue, then north on Temple Boulevard to Surf Avenue

5.____

6. While on patrol at Prospect Street and New York Avenue, Police Officers Ross and Rock are called to a burglary in progress near the entrance to the Apple-Terrace Co-ops on Poplar Street midway between Fine Avenue and Nostrand Boulevard.
Which one of the following is the SHORTEST route for them to take in their patrol car, making sure to obey all traffic regulations?
Travel _____ Poplar Street.

    A.   east on New York Avenue, then north
    B.   north on Prospect Avenue, then east on Fine Avenue, then south
    C.   north on Prospect Street, then east on Surf Avenue, then south
    D.   east on New York Avenue, then north on Temple Boulevard, then west on Surf Avenue, then south

6.____

Questions 7-8.

DIRECTIONS: Questions 7 and 8 are to be answered SOLELY on the basis of the map which appears below. The flow of traffic is indicated by the arrows. If there is only one arrow shown, then traffic flows only in the direction indicated by the arrow. If there are two arrows shown, then traffic flows in both directions. You must follow the flow of traffic.

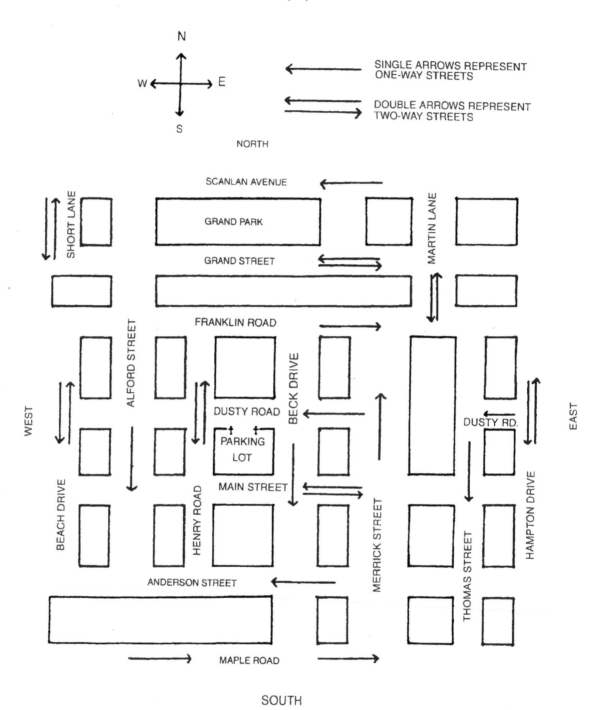

7. Police Officers Gold and Warren are at the intersection of Maple Road and Hampton Drive. The radio dispatcher has assigned them to investigate an attempted auto theft in the parking lot on Dusty Road.
Which one of the following is the SHORTEST route for the officers to take in their patrol car to get to the entrance of the parking lot on Dusty Road, making sure to obey all traffic regulations?
Travel _____ to the parking lot entrance.

7.____

A. north on Hampton Drive, then west on Dusty Road
B. west on Maple Road, then north on Beck Drive, then west on Dusty Road
C. north on Hampton Drive, then west on Anderson Street, then north on Merrick Street, then west on Dusty Road
D. west on Maple Road, then north on Merrick Street, then west on Dusty Road

8. Police Officer Gladden is in a patrol car at the intersection of Beach Drive and Anderson Street when he spots a suspicious car. Police Officer Gladden calls the radio dispatcher to determine if the vehicle was stolen. Police Officer Gladden then follows the vehicle north on Beach Drive for three blocks, then turns right and proceeds for one block and makes another right. He then follows the vehicle for two blocks, and then they both make a left turn and continue driving. Police Officer Gladden now receives a call from the dispatcher stating the car was reported stolen and signals for the vehicle to pull to the side of the road.
In what direction was Police Officer Gladden heading at the time he signaled for the other car to pull over?

8.____

A. North   B. East   C. South   D. West

Questions 9-10.

DIRECTIONS: Questions 9 and 10 are to be answered SOLELY on the basis of the map which appears on the following page. The flow of traffic is indicated by the arrows. If there is only one arrow shown, then traffic flows only in the direction indicated by the arrow. If there are two arrows shown, then traffic flows in both directions. You must follow the flow of traffic.

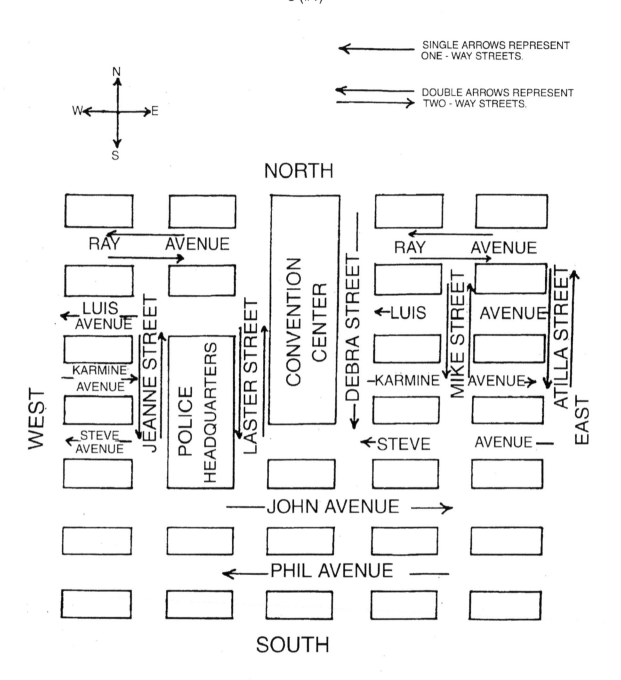

9. While in a patrol car located at Ray Avenue and Atilla Street, Police Officer Ashley
   receives a call from the dispatcher to respond to an assault at Jeanne Street and
   Karmine Avenue.
   Which one of the following is the SHORTEST route for Officer Ashley to follow in his
   patrol car, making sure to obey all traffic regulations?
   Travel

   A. south on Atilla Street, west on Luis Avenue, south on Debra Street, west on Steve
      Avenue, north on Lester Street, west on Luis Avenue, then one block south on
      Jeanne Street
   B. south on Atilla Street, then four blocks west on Phil Avenue, then north on Jeanne
      Street to Karmine Avenue

9._____

C. west on Ray Avenue to Debra Street, then five blocks south to Phil Avenue, then west to Jeanne Street, then three blocks north to Karmine Avenue

D. south on Atilla Street, then four blocks west on John Avenue, then north on Jeanne Street to Karmine Avenue

10. After taking a complaint report from the assault victim, Officer Ashley receives a call from the dispatcher to respond to an auto larceny in progress at the corner of Debra Street and Luis Avenue.
Which one of the following is the SHORTEST route for Officer Ashley to follow in his patrol car, making sure to obey all traffic regulations?
Travel

10.____

A. south on Jeanne Street to John Avenue, then east three blocks on John Avenue, then north on Mike Street to Luis Avenue, then west to Debra Street

B. south on Jeanne Street to John Avenue, then east two blocks on John Avenue, then north on Debra Street to Luis Avenue

C. north on Jeanne Street two blocks, then east on Ray Avenue for one block, then south on Lester Street to Steve Avenue, then one block east on Steve Avenue, then north on Debra Street to Luis Avenue

D. south on Jeanne Street to John Avenue, then east on John Avenue to Atilla Street, then north three blocks to Luis Avenue, then west to Debra Street

Questions 11-13.

DIRECTIONS: Questions 11 through 13 are to be answered SOLELY on the basis of the following map. The flow of traffic is indicated by the arrows. You must follow the flow of traffic.

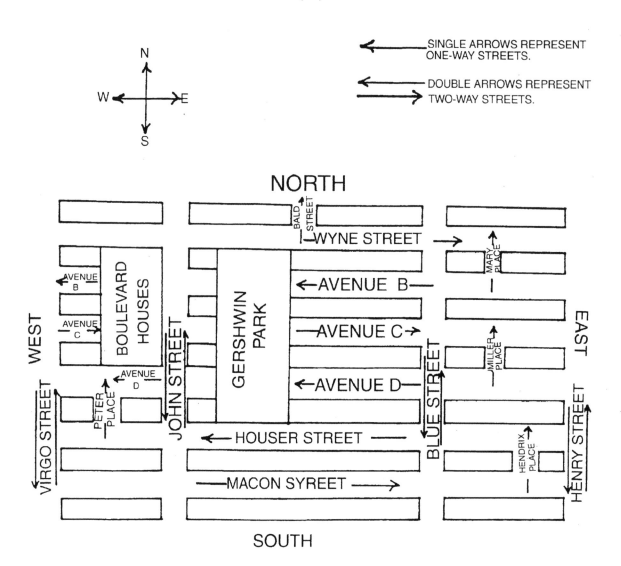

11. Police Officers Ranking and Fish are located at Wyne Street and John Street. The radio dispatcher has assigned them to investigate a motor vehicle accident at the corner of Henry Street and Houser Street.
Which one of the following is the SHORTEST route for them to take in their patrol car, making sure to obey all traffic regulations?
Travel

   A. four blocks south on John Street, then three blocks east on Houser Street to Henry Street

   B. two blocks east on Wyne Street, then two blocks south on Blue Street, then two blocks east on Avenue C, then two blocks south on Henry Street

   C. two blocks east on Wyne Street, then five blocks south on Blue Street, then two blocks east on Macon Street, then one block north on Henry Street

   D. five blocks south on John Street, then three blocks east on Macon Street, then one block north to Houser Street

11. ____

12. Police Officers Rizzo and Latimer are located at Avenue B and Virgo Street. They respond to the scene of a robbery at Miller Place and Avenue D.
Which one of the following is the SHORTEST route for them to take in their patrol car, making sure to obey all traffic regulations?
Travel _____ to Miller Place.

    A. one block north on Virgo Street, then four blocks east on Wyne Street, then three blocks south on Henry Street, then one block west on Avenue D

    B. four blocks south on Virgo Street, then two blocks east on Macon Street, then two blocks north on Blue Street, then one block east on Avenue D

    C. three blocks south on Virgo Street, then east on Houser Street to Henry Street, then one block north on Henry Street, then one block west on Avenue D

    D. four blocks south on Virgo Street, then four blocks east to Henry Street, then north to Avenue D, then one block west

12.____

13. Police Officer Bendix is in an unmarked patrol car at the intersection of John Street and Macon Street when he begins to follow a robbery suspect. The suspect goes one block east, turns left, travels for three blocks, and then turns right. He drives for two blocks and then makes a right turn. In the middle of the block, the suspect realizes he is being followed and makes a u-turn. In what direction is the suspect now headed?

    A. North   B. South   C. East   D. West

13.____

Questions 14-15.

DIRECTIONS: Questions 14 and 15 are to be answered SOLELY on the basis of the following map. The flow of traffic is indicated by the arrows. If there is only one arrow shown, then traffic flows only in the direction indicated by the arrow. If there are two arrows shown, then traffic flows in both directions. You must follow the flow of traffic.

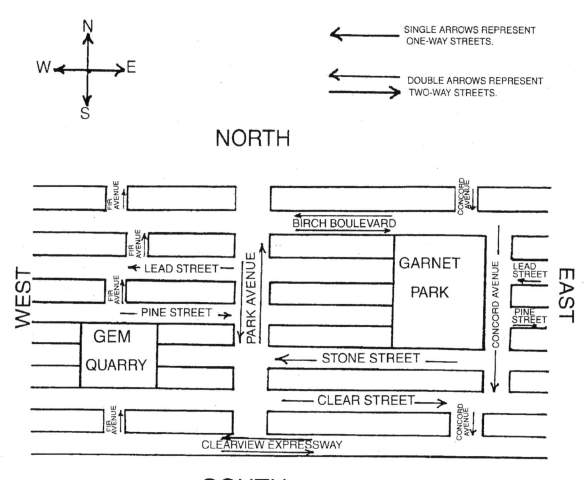

NORTH

SOUTH

14. You are located at Fir Avenue and Birch Boulevard and receive a request to respond to a   14._____
disturbance at Fir Avenue and Clear Street.
Which one of the following is the MOST direct route for you to take in your patrol car,
making sure to obey all traffic regulations?
Travel

A. one block east on Birch Boulevard, then four blocks south on Park Avenue, then
one block east on Clear Street
B. two blocks east on Birch Boulevard, then three blocks south on Concord Avenue,
then two blocks west on Stone Street, then one block south on Park Avenue, then
one block west on Clear Street
C. one block east on Birch Boulevard, then five blocks south on Park Avenue, then
one block west on the Clearview Expressway, then one block north on Fir Avenue
D. two blocks south on Fir Avenue, then one block east on Pine Street, then three
blocks south on Park Avenue, then one block east on the Clearview Expressway,
then one block north on Fir Avenue

15. You are located at the Clearview Expressway and Concord Avenue and receive a call to respond to a crime in progress at Concord Avenue and Pine Street. Which one of the following is the MOST direct route for you to take in your patrol car, making sure to obey all traffic regulations?
Travel

    15.____

    A. two blocks west on the Clearview Expressway, then one block north on Fir Avenue, then one block east on Clear Street, then four blocks north on Park Avenue, then one block east on Birch Boulevard, then two blocks south on Concord Avenue

    B. one block north on Concord Avenue, then one block west on Clear Street, then one block north on Park Avenue, then one block east on Stone Street, then one block north on Concord Avenue

    C. one block west on the Clearview Expressway, then four blocks north on Park Avenue, then one block west on Lead Street, then one block south on Fir Avenue

    D. one block west on the Clearview Expressway, then five blocks north on Park Avenue, then one block east on Birch Boulevard, then two blocks south on Concord Avenue

Questions 16-20.

DIRECTIONS: Questions 16 through 20 are to be answered SOLELY on the basis of the following map. The flow of traffic is indicated by the arrows. You must follow the flow of traffic.

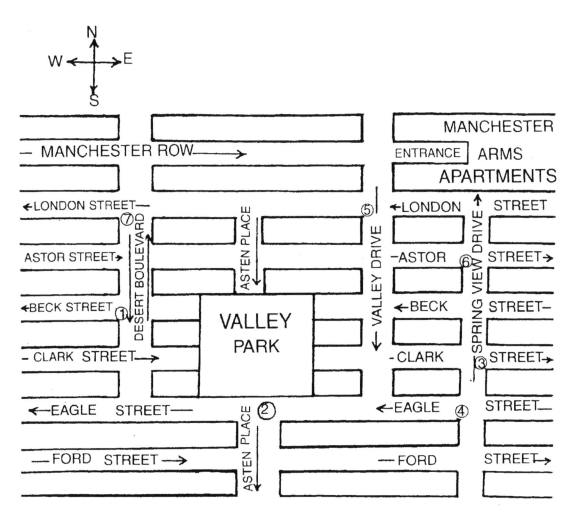

16. If you are located at Point 7 and travel south for one block, then turn east and travel two blocks, then turn south and travel two blocks, then turn east and travel one block, you will be CLOSEST to Point

    16._____

    A. 2   B. 3   C. 4   D. 6

17. If you are located at Point 3 and travel north for one block, and then turn west and travel one block, and then turn south and travel two blocks, and then turn west and travel one block, you will be CLOSEST to Point

    17._____

    A. 1   B. 2   C. 4   D. 6

18. You are located at Astor Street and Spring View Drive. You receive a call of a crime in progress at the intersection of Beck Street and Desert Boulevard.
    Which one of the following is the MOST direct route for you to take in your patrol car, making sure to obey all traffic regulations?
    Travel

    18._____

    A. one block north on Spring View Drive, then three blocks west on London Street, then two blocks south on Desert Boulevard
    B. three blocks west on Astor Street, then one block south on Desert Boulevard

C.   one block south on Spring View Drive, then three blocks west on Beck Street
D.   three blocks south on Spring View Drive, then three blocks west on Eagle Street, then two blocks north on Desert Boulevard

19.   You are located on Clark Street and Desert Boulevard and must respond to a disturbance at Clark Street and Spring View Drive.
Which one of the following is the MOST direct route for you to take in your patrol car, making sure to obey all traffic regulations?
Travel

    19.____

A.   two blocks north on Desert Boulevard, then three blocks east on Astor Street, then two blocks south on Spring View Drive
B.   one block south on Desert Boulevard, then three blocks east on Eagle Street, then one block north on Spring View Drive
C.   two blocks north on Desert Boulevard, then two blocks east on Astor Street, then three blocks south on Valley Drive, then one block east on Eagle Street, then one block north on Spring View Drive
D.   two blocks north on Desert Boulevard, then two blocks east on Astor Street, then two blocks south on Valley Drive, then one block east on Clark Street

20.   You are located at Valley Drive and Beck Street and receive a call to respond to the corner of Asten Place and Astor Street.
Which one of the following is the MOST direct route for you to take in your patrol car, making sure to obey all traffic regulations?
Travel _____ on Astor Street.

    20.____

A.   one block north on Valley Drive, then one block west
B.   two blocks south on Valley Drive, then one block east on Eagle Street, then three blocks north on Spring View Drive, then two blocks west
C.   two blocks south on Valley Drive, then two blocks west on Eagle Street, then three blocks north on Desert Boulevard, then one block east
D.   one block south on Valley Drive, then one block east on Clark Street, then two blocks north on Spring View Drive, then two blocks west

---

KEY (CORRECT ANSWERS)

1.	C		11.	B
2.	A		12.	A
3.	A		13.	A
4.	D		14.	C
5.	C		15.	D
6.	B		16.	B
7.	C		17.	B
8.	B		18.	A
9.	A		19.	D
10.	A		20.	C

MAP READING
EXAMINATION SECTION
TEST 1

DIRECTIONS: Each question or incomplete statement is followed by several suggested
answers or completions. Select the one that BEST answers the question or
completes the Statement. *PRINT THE LETTER OF THE CORRECT
ANSWER IN THE SPACE AT THE RIGHT.*

Questions 1-5.

DIRECTIONS: Questions 1 through 5 are to be answered SOLELY on the basis of the following information and map.

An employee may be required to assist civilians who seek travel directions or
referral to city agencies and facilities.

The following is a map of part of a city, where several public offices and other institutions
are located. Each of the squares represents one city block. Street names are as shown. If
there is an arrow next to the street name, it means the street is one-way only in the direction
of the arrow. If there is no arrow next to the street name, two-way traffic is allowed.

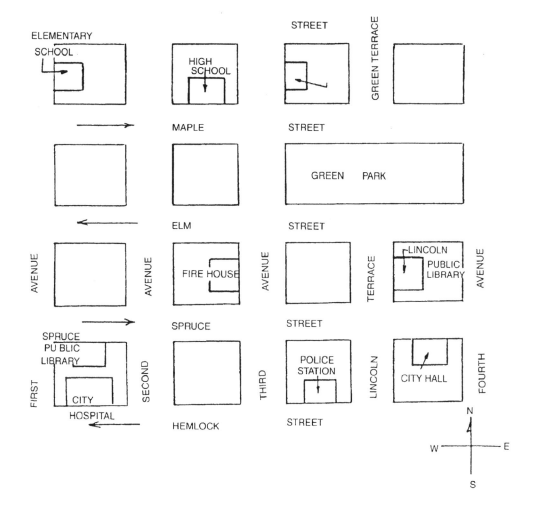

1. A woman whose handbag was stolen from her in Green Park asks a firefighter at the fire-   1.____
   house where to go to report the crime.
   The firefighter should tell the woman to go to the

   A. police station on Spruce Street
   B. police station on Hemlock Street
   C. city hall on Spruce Street
   D. city hall on Hemlock Street

2. A disabled senior citizen who lives on Green Terrace telephones the firehouse to ask   2.____
   which library is closest to her home.
   The firefighter should tell the senior citizen it is the

   A. Spruce Public Library on Lincoln Terrace
   B. Lincoln Public Library on Spruce Street
   C. Spruce Public Library on Spruce Street
   D. Lincoln Public Library on Lincoln Terrace

3. A woman calls the firehouse to ask for the exact location of City Hall.   3.____
   She should be told that it is on

   A. Hemlock Street, between Lincoln Terrace and Fourth Avenue
   B. Spruce Street, between Lincoln Terrace and Fourth Avenue
   C. Lincoln Terrace, between Spruce Street and Elm Street
   D. Green Terrace, between Maple Street and Pine Street

4. A delivery truck driver is having trouble finding the high school to make a delivery. The   4.____
   driver parks the truck across from the firehouse on Third Avenue facing north and goes
   into the firehouse to ask directions.
   In giving directions, the firefighter should tell the driver to go _____ to the school.

   A. north on Third Avenue to Pine Street and then make a right
   B. south on Third Avenue, make a left on Hemlock Street, and then make a right on
      Second Avenue
   C. north on Third Avenue, turn left on Elm Street, make a right on Second Avenue and
      go to Maple Street, then make another right
   D. north on Third Avenue to Maple Street, and then make a left

5. A man comes to the firehouse accompanied by his son and daughter. He wants to regis-   5.____
   ter his son in the high school and his daughter in the elementary school. He asks a firefighter which school is closest for him to walk to from the firehouse.
   The firefighter should tell the man that the

   A. high school is closer than the elementary school
   B. elementary school is closer than the high school
   C. elementary school and high school are the same distance away
   D. elementary school and high school are in opposite directions

Questions 6-8.

DIRECTIONS: Questions 6 through 8 are to be answered SOLELY on the basis of the following map and information. The flow of traffic is indicated by the arrows. If there is only one arrow shown, then traffic flows in the direction indicated by the arrow. If there are two arrows, then traffic flows in both directions. You must follow the flow of traffic

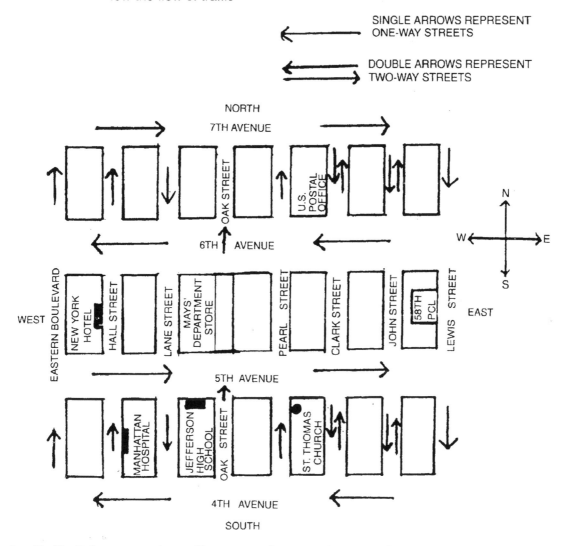

6. Traffic Enforcement Agent Fox was on foot patrol at John Street between 6th and 7th Avenues when a motorist driving southbound asked her for directions to the New York Hotel, which is located on Hall Street between 5th and 6th Avenues. Which one of the following is the SHORTEST route for Agent Fox to direct the motorist to take, making sure to obey all traffic regulations?

Travel _____ to the New York Hotel.

A. north on John Street, then east on 7th Avenue, then north on Lewis Street, then west on 4th Avenue, then north on Eastern Boulevard, then east on 5th Avenue, then north on Hall Street

B. south on John Street, then west on 6th Avenue, then south on Eastern Boulevard, then east on 5th Avenue, then north on Hall Street

6.____

C. south on John Street, then west on 6th Avenue, then south on Clark Street, then east on 4th Avenue, then north on Eastern Boulevard, then east on 5th Avenue, then north on Hall Street
D. south on John Street, then west on 4th Avenue, then north on Hall Street

7. Traffic Enforcement Agent Murphy is on motorized patrol on 7th Avenue between Oak Street and Pearl Street when Lt. Robertson radios him to go to Jefferson High School, located on 5th Avenue between Lane Street and Oak Street. Which one of the following is the SHORTEST route for Agent Murphy to take, making sure to obey all the traffic regulations?
Travel east on 7th Avenue, then south on _____, then east on 5th Avenue to Jefferson High School.

7._____

A. Clark Street, then west on 4th Avenue, then north on Hall Street
B. Pearl Street, then west on 4th Avenue, then north on Lane Street
C. Lewis Street, then west on 6th Avenue, then south on Hall Street
D. Lewis Street, then west on 4th Avenue, then north on Oak Street

8. Traffic Enforcement Agent Vasquez was on 4th Avenue and Eastern Boulevard when a motorist asked him for directions to the 58th Police Precinct, which is located on Lewis Street between 5th and 6th Avenues.
Which one of the following is the SHORTEST route for Agent Vasquez to direct the motorist to take, making sure to obey all traffic regulations.
Travel north on Eastern Boulevard, then east on _____ on Lewis Street to the 58th Police Precinct.

8._____

A. 5th Avenue, then north
B. 7th Avenue, then south
C. 6th Avenue, then north on Pearl Street, then east on 7th Avenue, then south
D. 5th Avenue, then north on Clark Street, then east on 6th Avenue, then south

Questions 9-13.

DIRECTIONS: Questions 9 through 13 are to be answered SOLELY on the basis of the following map and the following information.

Toll collectors answer motorists' questions concerning directions by reading a map of the metropolitan area. Although many alternate routes leading to destinations exist on the following map, you are to choose the MOST direct route of those given.

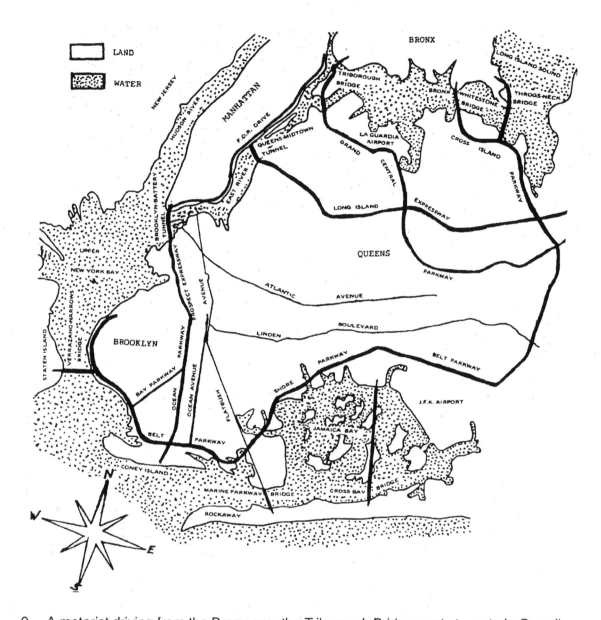

9. A motorist driving from the Bronx over the Triborough Bridge wants to go to LaGuardia Airport in Queens.
The officer should direct him to

   A. Grand Central Parkway   B. F.D.R. Drive
   C. Shore Parkway   D. Flatbush Avenue

9.____

10. A motorist driving from Manhattan through the Queens Midtown Tunnel would travel DIRECTLY onto

   A. Shore Parkway   B. F.D.R. Drive
   C. Long Island Expressway   D. Atlantic Avenue

10.____

11. A motorist traveling north over the Marine Parkway Bridge should take which route to reach Coney Island?

   A. Shore Parkway East   B. Belt Parkway West
   C. Linden Boulevard   D. Ocean Parkway

11.____

12. Which facility does NOT connect the Bronx and Queens? 12.____

    A. Triborough Bridge   B. Bronx-Whitestone Bridge
    C. Verrazano-Narrows Bridge   D. Throgs-Neck Bridge

13. A motorist driving from Manhattan arrives at the toll booth of the Brooklyn-Battery Tunnel 13.____
    and asks directions to Ocean Parkway.
    To which one of the following routes should the motorist FIRST be directed?

    A. Atlantic Avenue   B. Bay Parkway
    C. Prospect Expressway   D. Ocean Avenue

Questions 14-16.

DIRECTIONS: Questions 14 through 16 are to be answered SOLELY on the basis of the fol-
                 lowing map. The flow of traffic is indicated by the arrows. If there is only one
                 arrow shown, then traffic flows only in the direction indicated by the arrow. If
                 there are two arrows, then traffic flows in both directions. You must follow the
                 flow of traffic.

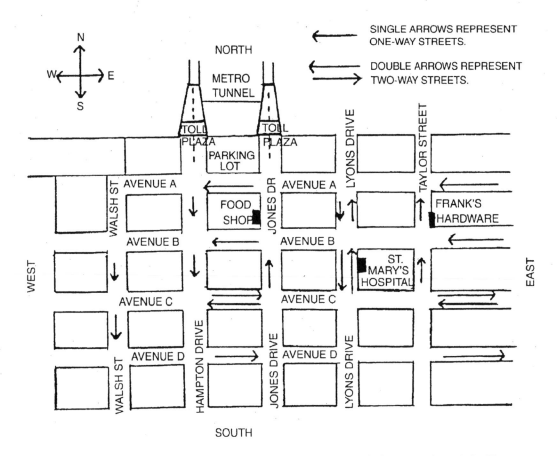

14. A motorist is exiting the Metro Tunnel and approaches the bridge and tunnel officer at the 14.____
    toll plaza. He asks the officer how to get to the food shop on Jones Drive. Which one of
    the following is the SHORTEST route for the motorist to take, making sure to obey all
    traffic regulations?
    Travel south on Hampton Drive, then left on _____ on Jones Drive to the food shop.

A.   Avenue A, then right   B.   Avenue B, then right
C.   Avenue D, then left   D.   Avenue C, then left

15.   A motorist heading south pulls up to a toll booth at the exit of the Metro Tunnel and asks   15.____
      Bridge and Tunnel Officer Evans how to get to Frank's Hardware Store on Taylor Street.
      Which one of the following is the SHORTEST route for the motorist to take, making
      sure to obey all traffic regulations?
      Travel south on Hampton Drive, then east on

      A.   Avenue B to Taylor Street
      B.   Avenue D, then north on Taylor Street to Avenue B
      C.   Avenue C, then north on Taylor Street to Avenue B
      D.   Avenue C, then north on Lyons Drive, then east on Avenue B to Taylor Street

16.   A motorist is exiting the Metro Tunnel and approaches the toll plaza. She asks Bridge   16.____
      and Tunnel Officer Owens for directions to St. Mary's Hospital.
      Which one of the following is the SHORTEST route for the motorist to take, making
      sure to obey all traffic regulations?
      Travel south on Hampton Drive, then _____ on Lyons Drive to St. Mary's Hospital.

      A.   left on Avenue D, then left
      B.   right on Avenue A, then left on Walsh Street, then left on Avenue D, then left
      C.   left on Avenue C, then left
      D.   left on Avenue B, then right

Questions 17-18.

DIRECTIONS: Questions 17 and 18 are to be answered SOLELY on the basis of the map
                which appears on the following page. The flow of traffic is indicated by the
                arrows. If there is only one arrow shown, then traffic flows only in the direction
                indicated by the arrow. If there are two arrows shown, then traffic flows in both
                directions. You must follow the flow of traffic.

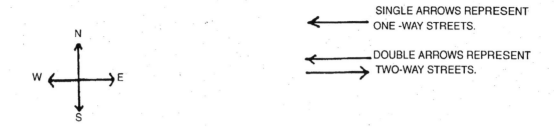

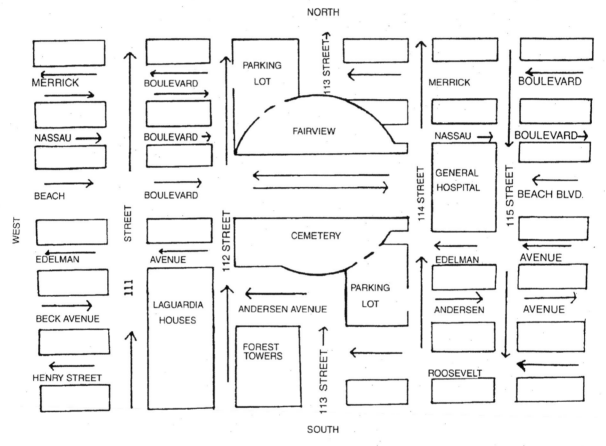

17. Police Officers Glenn and Albertson are on 111th Street at Henry Street when they are dispatched to a past robbery at Beach Boulevard and 115th Street.
Which one of the following is the SHORTEST route for the officers to follow in their patrol car, making sure to obey all traffic regulations?
Travel north on lllth Street, then east on _____ south on 115th Street.

17.____

   A. Edelman Avenue, then north on 112th Street, then east on Beach Boulevard, then north on 114th Street, then east on Nassau Boulevard, then one block
   B. Beach Boulevard, then north on 114th Street, then east on Nassau Boulevard, then one block
   C. Merrick Boulevard, then two blocks
   D. Nassau Boulevard, then south on 112th Street, then east on Beach Boulevard, then north on 114th Street, then east on Nassau Boulevard, then one block

18. Later in their tour, Officers Glenn and Albertson are driving on 114th Street.   18._____
     If they make a left turn to enter the parking lot at Andersen Avenue, and then make a
     u-turn, in what direction would they now be headed?

     A. North   B. South   C. East   D. West

Questions 19-20.

DIRECTIONS: Questions 19 and 20 are to be answered SOLELY on the basis of the following
               map. The flow of traffic is indicated by the arrows. If there is only one arrow
               shown, then traffic flows only in the direction indicated by the arrow. If there are
               two arrows shown, then traffic flows in both directions. You must follow the flow
               of traffic.

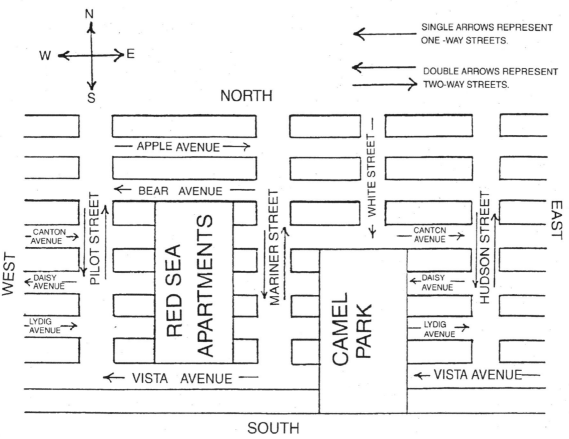

19. You are located at Apple Avenue and White Street. You receive a call to respond to the   19._____
     corner of Lydig Avenue and Pilot Street.
     Which one of the following is the MOST direct route for you to take in your patrol car,
     making sure to obey all traffic regulations?
     Travel _____ on Pilot Street.

     A. two blocks south on White Street, then one block east on Canton Avenue, then one
         block north on Hudson Street, then three blocks west on Bear Avenue, then three
         blocks south
     B. one block south on White Street, then two blocks west on Bear Avenue, then three
         blocks south

C. two blocks west on Apple Avenue, then four blocks south
D. two blocks south on White Street, then one block west on Canton Avenue, then three blocks south on Mariner Street, then one block west on Vista Avenue, then one block north

20. You are located at Canton Avenue and Pilot Street. You receive a call of a crime in progress at the intersection of Canton Avenue and Hudson Street.
Which one of the following is the MOST direct route for you to take in your patrol car, making sure to obey all traffic regulations?
Travel   20.____

A. two blocks north on Pilot Street, then two blocks east on Apple Avenue, then one block south on White Street, then one block east on Bear Avenue, then one block south on Hudson Street
B. three blocks south on Pilot Street, then travel one block east on Vista Avenue, then travel three blocks north on Mariner Street, then travel two blocks east on Canton Avenue
C. one block north on Pilot Street, then travel three blocks east on Bear Avenue, then travel one block south on Hudson Street
D. two blocks north on Pilot Street, then travel three blocks east on Apple Avenue, then travel two blocks south on Hudson Street

---

KEY (CORRECT ANSWERS)

1.	B	11.	B/D
2.	D	12.	C
3.	B	13.	C
4.	C	14.	D
5.	A	15.	C
6.	D	16.	C
7.	A	17.	B
8.	B	18.	C
9.	A	19.	B
10.	C	20.	D

FOLLOWING ORAL DIRECTIONS

COMMENTARY

A large part of any job is listening to the supervisor and following his instructions. Since it is important that each employee do exactly as he is instructed, this test is used to make sure that each applicant can and will listen carefully and follow through without extra supervision.

The directions in the test are not hard to follow, but you must listen carefully and do exactly what you are told to do.

In order to do this practice section, you must have a friend who will read the directions to you. *Do not read the material in this section yourself; if you do, you will lose the value of this practice.*

DESCRIPTION OF THE TEST

FOLLOWING ORAL DIRECTIONS - SAMPLE QUESTIONS

The directions are to be read at the rate of 80 words per minute. Since not everybody speaks at this speed, your friend should practice reading the 1-minute practice that follows until he can read it in exactly 1 minute whenever he wants to. He will also need a watch with a second hand. Give the 1-Minute Practice box to your friend to use. (Each friend who is helping you will have to use it to practice, so don't throw it away.)

FOR THE PERSON WHO WILL READ THE FOLLOWING ORAL DIRECTIONS TEST TO YOU

The directions should be read at about 80 words per minute. Practice reading aloud the material in the box below until you can do it in exactly 1 minute. This will give you a feel for the way you should read the test material.

1-MINUTE PRACTICE
(This is for practice in reading aloud. It is not the sample test.)

> Look at line 20 in your work booklet. There are two circles and two boxes of different sizes with numbers in them. If 7 is less than 3 and if 2 is smaller than 4, write a G in the larger circle. Otherwise write B as in baker in the smaller box. Now on your Code Sheet darken the space for the number-letter combination in the box or circle.

When your friend reads the directions to you, listen carefully and do what he says. If you fall behind and miss a direction, don't get
excited. Let that one go and listen for the next one. Since B and D sound very much alike, he will say "B as in baker" when he means B and "D as in dog" when he means D.

He will tell you some things to do with the 5 sample questions below. Then, when he tells you to darken a box on the Sample Answer Sheet, use the one on this page.

SAMPLE QUESTIONS

SAMPLE QUESTIONS

QUESTION 1. 5————

QUESTION 2. 1 6 4 3 7

QUESTION 3. D B A E C

QUESTION 4. (8—) (5—) (2—) (9—) (10—)

QUESTION 5. (7—) [6—] (1—) [12—]

SAMPLE ANSWER SHEET

DIRECTIONS to be read. (The words in parentheses should *not* be read aloud. They tell you how long you should pause at the various spots. You should time the pauses with a watch with a second hand. The instruction "Pause slightly" means that you should stop long enough to take a breath.) You should not repeat any directions.

QUESTIONS ON THE SAMPLE

You are to follow the instructions that I read to you. I cannot repeat them.

Look at the Sample Questions. Question 1 has a number and a line beside it. On the line write an A.(Pause 2 seconds.) Now on the Sample Answer Sheet, find number 5 (pause 2 seconds) and darken the box for the letter you just wrote on the line. (Pause 5 seconds.)
Look at Question 2. (Pause slightly.) Draw a line under the third number. (Pause 2 seconds.) Now on the Sample Answer Sheet, find the number under which you just drew a line and darken box B as in baker for that number. (Pause 5 seconds.)

Look at the letters in Question 3. (Pause slightly.) Draw a line under the third letter in the line. (Pause 2 seconds.) Now on your . answer sheet, find number 9 (pause 2 seconds) and darken the box for the letter under which you drew a line. (Pause 5 seconds.)

Look at the five circles in Question 4. (Pause slightly.) Each circle has a number and a line in it. Write D as in dog on the blank in the last circle. (Pause 2 seconds.) Now on the Sample Answer Sheet, darken the space for the number-letter combination that is in the circle you just wrote in. (Pause 5 seconds.)

Look at Question 5. (Pause slightly.) There are two circles and two boxes of different sizes with numbers in them. (Pause slightly.) If 4 is more than 2 and if 5 is less than 3, write A in the smaller circle. (Pause slightly.) Otherwise write C in the larger box. (Pause 2 seconds.) Now on the Sample Answer Sheet, darken the space for the number-letter combination in the box or circle in which you just wrote. (Pause 5 seconds.)

Now look at the Sample Answer Sheet. (Pause slightly.) You should have darkened spaces 4B, 5A, 9A, 10D, and 12C on the Sample Answer Sheet.

SUGGESTIONS FOR DOING THE TEST OF FOLLOWING ORAL DIRECTIONS

* Listen carefully to the directions.
* Do exactly what the examiner tells you to do.
* Do not try to get ahead of the examiner.
* If you missed an instruction, wait for the next one.
* Make sure that you darken ONLY one box for each number on the answer sheet.

EXAMINATION SECTION
TEST 1

NOTE: In the examinations the examiner will read aloud directions for you to follow. A sample of directions is given below. The directions are not the same as the directions in the test, but they are somewhat alike. You should have a sheet of lined paper and a pencil as well as the Answer Sheet before you begin.

DIRECTIONS:
1. Fold your lined paper into 4 columns. (Pause for examinee to do this.)
2. In the first column, on the first line, write the number 4. (Pause)
3. On the second line in the same column, write the number 15.
4. Next line, write 12. (Pause)
5. Now go to column 2.
6. Write 35 on the first line (Pause), 26 on the next line, (Pause), and 38 on the third line. (Pause)
7. In column 3, write 11 on the first line (Pause), 18 on the next line (Pause) and 6 last.
8. In column 4, write 16 on the first line next to 4, (Pause), 32 next (Pause) and 19 last.
9. The first number in the first column is 4.
10. Write the letter C next to 4, so it reads 4C. (Pause)
11. The first number in the second column is 35.
12. Write the same letter next to it, so it reads 35C. (Pause)
13. Write C next to the other numbers on the first line, so they read 11C (Pause) and 16C. (Pause)
14. Write the letter A next to each number on the second line, so they read 15A, 26A, etc. (Pause)
15. Write the letter B as in Boy next to each number on the third line. (Pause)
16. Now, take the Answer Sheet you cut out.
17. It has numbers from 1 to 40, and letter spaces.
18. You will mark one space for certain numbers.
19. See how D has been marked for number 1.
20. You will make the same kind of black mark where I tell you. (Pause)
21. Mark 2E. That is, make a black mark at space E for number 2. (Pause)
22. Mark 9C. (Pause)
23. Mark 26C. (Pause)
24. Mark B as in Boy for 15, 16, and 20. (Pause)
25. Mark E for 12, 29, 34, and 39- (Pause)
26. Remember you should *NOT* have more than one mark for any number.
27. If I call a *SECOND* letter for a number where you already have a letter, do *NOT* mark the,new letter. Instead, mark the letter A for the number below It.
28. Now I call 2D . You should *1301* mark 2D, because you have already marked 2E. Instead, mark A for the next number.
29. The next number to 2 is 3. So, you should mark 3A. (Pause)
30. Remember to mark A for the *NEXT* number to the one I call if I call a number where you already have a mark.
31. Now I call 28C. (Pause)
32. Next, 9B. (Pause)
33. 17C. (Pause)
34. 12D. (Pause)

35. 26E and 29D. (Pause)
36. Now, take the sheet of lined paper on which you wrote letters and, numbers. (Pause)
37. You will mark the space on your answer sheet for each number and letter you wrote. For example, the first is 4C, so you will mark 4C on your answer sheet .
38. Do *NOT* start until I tell you.
39. Remember: if you have a mark *ALREADY MADE* for a number, do *NOT* mark another letter. If there is already a mark for a number, make *NO* new mark at all.
40. Start to mark, now!

KEY (CORRECT ANSWERS)

1.		11.	C	21.		31.	
2.	E	12.	E	22.		32.	A
3.	A	13.	A	23.		33.	
4.	C	14.		24.		34.	E
5.		15.	B	25.		35.	C
6.	B	16.	B	26.	C	36.	
7.		17.	C	27.	A	37.	
8.		18.	A	28.	C	38.	B
9.	C	19.	B	29.	E	39.	E
10.	A	20.	B	30.	A	40.	

NOTE: ANY OTHER MARK COUNTS AS WRONG. YOU LOSE CREDIT FOR EACH WRONG MARK.

TEST 2

DIRECTIONS: In the test that follows the examiner will read directions aloud and you will mark your -answer sheet as directed.

1.   "Mark E for *82,* 83, 85, (slight pause) 78, and 102. (Pause)
2.   "Mark C for 107, 110, and 103. (Pause)
3.   "Mark D as in dog for 101, 110, (slight pause) 76, and 85. (Pause)

"For the next set of questions, mark space E and also mark the letter I call, unless E is already marked. If E is already marked for that number, do not make any mark for that number.

4.   "Mark B as in boy for 106, 78, (slight pause) 80, and 84 . (Pause)
5.   "Mark A for 108, 104, 83, and 109. (Pause)
6.   "Mark C for 79, 102, (slight pause) and 77."

———

KEY (CORRECT ANSWERS)

76.	D	86.		96.		106.	B, E
77.	C, E	87.		97.		107.	C
78.	E	88.		98.		108.	A, E
79.	C, E	89.		99.		109.	A, E
80.	B, E	90.		100.		110.	C, D

81.		91.		101.	D
82.	E	92.		102.	E
83.	E	93.		103.	C
84.	B, E	94.		104.	A, E
85.	D, E	95.		105.	

NOTE: ANY OTHER MARK COUNTS AS WRONG. YOU LOSE CREDIT FOR EACH WRONG MARK.

—————

TEST 3

DIRECTIONS: 1. "Mark B as in boy for 29, 12, 17, 38, 8 . (Pause)
2. "Mark D as in dog for 13, 6, 24, 5. (Pause)
3. "Mark A for 40, 27, 1, 15, 9. (Pause)
4. "Mark E for 13, 39, 31, 4, and 10. (Pause)

"For the next set of questions, mark space E and also mark the letter I call, unless E is already marked. If E is already marked for that number, do *NOT* make any mark for that number.

5. "Mark D as in dog for 12, 9, 19, 23, 2. (Pause)
6. "Mark C for 31, 37, 4, 39. (Pause)
7. "Mark B as in boy for 21, 16, 7, 10, and 26."

KEY (CORRECT ANSWERS)

1.	A	11.		21.	B, E	31.	E
2.	D, E	12.	B, D, E	22.		32.	
3.		13.	D, E	23.	D, E	33.	
4.	E	14.		24.	D	34.	
5.	D	15.	A	25.		35.	
6.	D	16.	B, E	26.	B, E	36.	
7.	B, E	17.	B	27.	A	37.	C, E
8.	B	18.		28.		38.	B
9.	A, D, E	19.	D, E	29.	B	39.	E
10.	E	20.		30.		40.	A

NOTE: ANY OTHER MARK COUNTS AS WRONG. YOU LOSE CREDIT FOR EACH
WRONG MARK.

———

TEST 4

DIRECTIONS:
1. "Mark A for 59, 33, 44, 66, and 75- (Pause)
2. "Mark B as in boy for 69, 42, 31, and 72. (Pause)
3. "Mark E for 35, 64, 58, 47, and 61. (Pause)

"For the next set of questions, mark space B and also mark the letter I call, unless B is already marked. If B is already marked for that number, do *NOT* mark the new letter. Instead, mark the letter B for the number below it .

4. "Mark D as in dog for 32, 41, 70, and 63. (Pause)
5. "Mark C for 44, 48, 37, 74, and 37 (Pause)
6. "Mark E for 72, 67, 60, 42, and 46. (Pause)
7. "Mark A for 34, 56, 67, 38, and 71."

———————

KEY (CORRECT ANSWERS)

31.	B	46.	B, E	61.	E
32.	B, D	47.	E	62.	
33.	A	48.	B, C	63.	B, D
34.	A, B	49.		64.	E
35.	E	50.		65.	
36.		51.		66.	A
37.	B, C	52.		67.	B, E
38.	B	53.		68.	B
39.	B	54.		69.	B
40.		55.		70.	B, D
41.	B, D	56.	A, B	71.	A, B
42.	B	57.		72.	B
43.	B	58.	E	73.	B
44.	A, B, C	59.	A	74.	B, C
45.		60.	B, E	75.	A

NOTE: ANY OTHER MARK COUNTS AS WRONG. YOU LOSE CREDIT FOR EACH WRONG MARK.

TEST 5

DIRECTIONS:
1. "Mark C for 73, 96, 84, and 80. (Pause)
2. "Mark D as in dog for 68, 88, 99, 91, 78, and 67. (Pause)
3. "Mark E for 70, 93, 82, 75, and 92. (Pause)
4. "Mark B as in boy for 87, 69, 77, 98, and 71. (Pause)

"For the next set of questions, mark space C and also mark the letter I call, unless C is already marked. If C is already marked for that number, do *NOT* mark the new letter. Instead mark the letter A for the number below it.

5. "Mark D as in dog for 72, 89, 92, and 84. (Pause)
6. "Mark A for 66, 95, 77, and 73. (Pause)
7. "Mark B as in boy for 75, 83, 88, 90, 96, 100, and 94."

KEY (CORRECT ANSWERS)

66.	A, C	76.		86.		96.	C
67.	D	77.	A, B, C	87.	B	97.	A
68.	D	78.	D	88.	B, C, D	98.	B
69.	B	79.	C, D	89.	C, D	99.	D
70.	E	80.	C	90.	B, C	100.	B, C
71.	B	81.		91.	D		
72.	C, D	82.	C, D, E	92.	E		
73.	C	83.	B, C	93.	E		
74.	A	84.	C	94.	B, C		
75.	B, C, E	85.	A	95.	A, C		

NOTE: ANY OTHER MARK COUNTS AS WRONG. YOU LOSE CREDIT FOR EACH
WRONG MARK.

TEST 6

DIRECTIONS: 1. "Mark E for 50, 37, 19, 24, and 11. (Pause)
2. "Mark B as in boy for 16, 22, 40, and 31. (Pause)
3. "Mark D as in dog for 24, 40, 49, 33,' and 17. (Pause)

"For the next set of questions, mark space D as in dog and also mark the letter I call, unless D is already marked. If D is already marked for that number, do *NOT* mark the new letter. Instead mark the letter E for the number above it.

4. "Mark C for 12, 21, 42, and 29. (Pause)
5. "Mark A for 19, 49, 24, 15, 47, and 40. (Pause)
6. "Mark E for 41, 34, 29, and 17."

———

KEY (CORRECT ANSWERS)

10.		20.		30.		40.	B, D
11.	E	21.	C, D	31.	B	41.	D, E
12.	C, D	22.	B	32.		42.	C, D
13.		23.	E	33.	D	43.	
14.		24.	D, E	34.	D, E	44.	
15.	A, D	25.		35.		45.	
16.	B, E	26.		36.		46.	
17.	D	27.		37.	E	47.	A, D
18.		28.	E	38.		48.	E
19.	A, D, E	29.	C, D	39.	E	49.	D
						50.	E

NOTE: ANY OTHER MARK COUNTS AS WRONG. YOU LOSE CREDIT FOR EACH WRONG MARK.

TEST 7

DIRECTIONS:
1. "Mark D as in dog for 79, 51, 69, 42, and 64.(Pause)
2. "Mark A for 44, 62, 51, 59, 50, 42, 76, and 67. (Pause)
3. "Mark C for 64, 73, 80, 49, 55, and 62. (Pause)

"For the next set of questions, mark space A and also the letter I call, unless A is already marked. If A is already marked for that number, do *NOT* mark the new letter. Instead mark the letter E for that number.

4. "Mark E for 74, 68, 41, 77, and 58. (Pause)
5. "Mark B as in boy for 67, 60, 78, 44, and 76. (Pause)
6. "Mark C for 60, 51, 48, 69, 56, 66, and 79."

———

KEY (CORRECT ANSWERS)

41.	A, E	51.	A, D, E	61.		71.	
42.	A, D	52.		62.	A, C	72.	
43.		53.		63.		73.	C
44.	A, E	54.		64.	C, D	74.	A, E
45.		55.	C	65.		75.	
46.		56.	A, C	66.	A, C	76.	A, E
47.		57.		67.	A, E	77.	A, E
48.	A, C	58.	A, E	68.	A, E	78.	A, B
49.	C	59.	A	69.	A, C, D	79.	A, C, D
50.	A	60.	A, B, E	70.		80.	C

NOTE: ANY OTHER MARK COUNTS AS WRONG. YOU LOSE CREDIT FOR EACH WRONG MARK.

———

TEST 8

DIRECTIONS: 1. "Mark C for 37, 8, 29, 23, and 46. (Pause)
                 2. "Mark E for 50, 4 0, 28, 3, and 29. (Pause)
                 3. "Mark B as in boy for 38, 26, 23, 45, 47, and 35- (Pause)

"For the next set of questions, mark space C and also the letter I call, unless C... is already marked. If C is already marked for that number, do NOT mark the new letter. Instead mark the letter B for the number that is <u>two below</u> it. V-

                 4. "Mark D as in dog for 48, 14, 8, 23, 33, 18, and 34. (Pause)
                 5. "Mark A for 42, 2, 16, 43, and 29. (Pause)
                 6. "Mark E for 4, 41, 48, and 15."

KEY (CORRECT ANSWERS)

1.		16.	A, C	31.	B	46.	C
2.	A, C	17.		32.		47.	B
3.	E	18.	C, D	33.	C, D	48.	C, D
4.	C, E	19.		34.	C, D	49.	
5.		20.		35.	B	50.	B, E
6.		21.		36.			
7.		22.		37.	C		
8.	C	23.	B, C	38.	B		
9.		24.		39.			
10.	B	25.	B	40.	E		
11.		26.	B	41.	C, E		
12.		27.		42.	A, C		
13.		28.	E	43.	A, C		
14.	C, D	29.	C, E	44.			
15.	C, E	30.		45.	B		

NOTE: ANY OTHER MARK COUNTS AS WRONG. YOU LOSE CREDIT FOR EACH WRONG MARK.

___

TEST 9

DIRECTIONS:
1. "Mark A for 87, 56, 95, 98, 99, 54, 63, and 59. (Pause)
2. "Mark D as in dog for 84, 100, 57, 68, 87, and 60. (Pause)
3. "Mark C for 70, 52, 69, 96, 78, 84, 58, 53, 68, and 76. (Pause)

"For the next set of questions, mark space A and also mark the letter I call, unless A is already marked. If A is already marked for that number, do *NOT* mark the new letter. Instead mark the letter E for the number that is <u>two above</u> it.

4. "Mark B as in boy for 89, 51, 66, 73, 62, and 98. (Pause)
5. "Mark E for 55, 71, 90, 87, 65, 99, and 66. (Pause)
6. "Mark D as in dog for 75, 91, 80, 54, 89, and 95."

———

KEY (CORRECT ANSWERS)

51.	A, B	66.	A, B	81.		96.	C, E
52.	C, E	67.		82.		97.	E
53.	C	68.	C, D	83.		98.	A
54.	A	69.	C	84.	C, D	99.	A
55.	A, E	70.	C	85.	E	100.	D
56.	A	71.	A, E	86.			
57.	D	72.		87.	A, D, E		
58.	C	73.	A, B	88.			
59.	A	74.		89.	A, B		
60.	D	75.	A, D	90.	A, E		
61.		76.	C	91.	A, D		
62.	A, B	77.		92.			
63.	A	78.	C	93.	E		
64.	E	79.		94.			
65.	A,E	80.	A, D	95.	A		

NOTE: ANY OTHER MARK COUNTS AS WRONG. YOU LOSE CREDIT FOR EACH WRONG MARK.

TEST 10

DIRECTIONS:
1. "Mark E for 87, 12, 93, 29, 9, 94, 16, .33, 21, 59, 67, 43, and 17. (Pause)
2. "Mark C for 82, 7, 63, 37, 97, 55, 39, 5, 47, and 25 (Pause)
3. "Mark B as in boy for 89, 66, 77, 35, 92, 18, 54, 13, 71, and 30. (Pause)

"For the next set of questions, mark space E and also mark the letter I call unless E is already marked. If E is already marked for that number, do *NOT* mark the new letter. Instead mark the letter D for the number that is three above it and the letter A for the number that is three below it.

4. "Mark A for 91, 62, 14, 87, and 33. (Pause)
5. "Mark B as in boy for 51, 11, 98, 51, 68, and 9. (Pause)
6. Mark C for 56, 4l, 28, 94, 43, and 29."

———————

KEY (CORRECT ANSWERS)

1.		26.	D	51.	D, E	76.	
2.		27.		52.		77.	B
3.		28.	C, E	53.		78.	
4.		29.	E	54.	A, B	79.	
5.	C	30.	B, D	55.	C	80.	
6.	D	31.		56.	C, E	81.	
7.	C	32.	A	57.		82.	C
8.		33.	E	58.		83.	
9.	E	34.		59.	E	84.	D
10.		35.	B	60.		85.	
11.	D, E	36.	A	61.		86.	
12.	A, E	37.	C	62.	A, E	87.	E
13.	B	38.		63.	C	88.	
14.	A, E	39.	C	64.		89.	B
15.		40.	D	65.		90.	A
16.	E	41.	C, E	66.	B	91.	A, D, E
17.	E	42.		67.	E	92.	B
18.	B	43.	E	68.	D, E	93.	E
19.		44.		69.		94.	E
20.		45.		70.		95.	
21.	E	46.	A	71.	B	96.	
22.		47.	C	72.		97.	A, C
23.		48.	D	73.		98.	D, E
24.		49.		74.		99.	
25.	C	50.		75.		100.	

NOTE: ANY OTHER MARK COUNTS AS WRONG. YOU LOSE CREDIT FOR EACH WRONG MARK.

MECHANICAL APTITUDE
MECHANICAL COMPREHENSION
EXAMINATION SECTION
TEST 1

DIRECTIONS : Each question or incomplete statement below is followed by several suggested answers or completions. Select the *one* that *BEST* answers the question or completes the statement. *PRINT THE LETTER OF THE CORRECT ANSWER IN THE SPACE AT THE RIGHT.*

Questions 1-3.

DIRECTIONS: Questions 1 to 3 inclusive are based upon the following paragraph.

The only openings permitted in fire partitions except openings for ventilating ducts shall be those required for doors. There shall be but one such door opening unless the provision of additional openings would not exceed, in total width of all doorways, 25 percent of the length of the wall. The minimum distance between openings shall be three feet. The maximum area for such a door opening shall be 80 square feet, except that such openings for the passage of motor trucks may be a maximum of 140 square feet.

1. According to the above paragraph, openings in fire partitions are permitted *only* for

    A. doors
    B. doors and windows
    C. doors and ventilation ducts
    D. doors, windows and ventilation ducts

1 _____

2. In a fire partition, 22 feet long and 10 feet high, the *MAXIMUM* number of doors, 3 feet wide and 7 feet high, is

    A. 1   B. 2   C. 3   D. 4

2 _____

3.

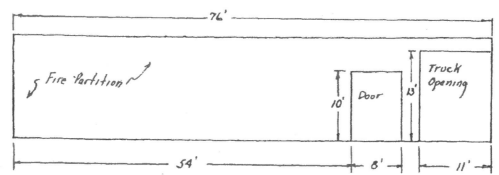

The **one** of the following statements about the layout shown above that is *MOST* accurate is that the

    A. total width of the openings is too large
    B. truck opening is too large
    C. truck and door openings are too close together
    D. layout is acceptable

3 _____

4. At a given temperature, a wet hand will freeze to a bar of metal, but *NOT* to a piece of   4____
   wood, because the

   A. metal expands and contracts more than the wood
   B. wood is softer than the metal
   C. wood will burn at a lower temperature than the metal
   D. metal is a better conductor of heat than the wood

5. Of the following items commonly found in a household, the one that uses the *MOST* elec-   5____
   tric current is a(n)

   A. 150-watt light bulb   B. toaster
   C. door buzzer   D. 8" electric fan

6. Sand and ashes are frequently placed on icy pavements to prevent skidding. The effect   6____
   of the sand and ashes is to increase

   A. inertia   B. gravity   C. momentum   D. friction

7. The air near the ceiling of a room usually is warmer than the air near the floor because   7____

   A. there is better air circulation at the floor level
   B. warm air is lighter than cold air
   C. windows usually are nearer the floor than the ceiling
   D. heating pipes usually run along the ceiling

8.   8____

Dɪᴀ. 1   Dɪᴀ. 2

It is safer to use the ladder positioned as shown in diagram 1 than as shown in diagram
2 because, in diagram 1,

   A. less strain is placed upon the center rungs of the ladder
   B. it is easier to grip and stand on the ladder
   C. the ladder reaches a lower height
   D. the ladder is less likely to tip over backwards

9.

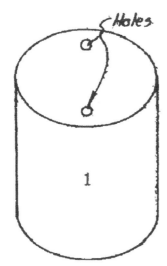

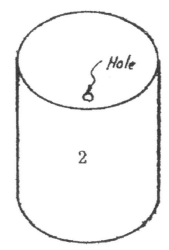

9____

It is *easier* to pour a liquid from:

A. Can 1 because there are two holes from which the liquid can flow
B. Can 1 because air can enter through one hole while the liquid comes out the other hole
C. Can 2 because the liquid comes out under greater pressure
D. Can 2 because it is easier to direct the flow of the liquid when there is only one hole

10. A substance which is subject to "spontaneous combustion" is one that   10____

A. is explosive when heated
B. is capable of catching fire without an external source of heat
C. acts to speed up the burning of material
D. liberates oxygen when heated

11. The sudden shutting down of a nozzle on a hose discharging water under high pressure   11____
is a *bad* practice *CHIEFLY* because the

A. hose is likely to whip about violently
B. hose is likely to burst
C. valve handle is likely to snap
D. valve handle is likely to jam

12. Fire can continue where there are present fuel, oxygen from the air or other source, and   12____
a sufficiently high temperature to maintain combustion. The method of extinguishment of
fire *MOST* commonly used is to

A. remove the fuel
B. exclude the oxygen from the burning material
C. reduce the temperature of the burning material
D. smother the flames of the burning material

13.

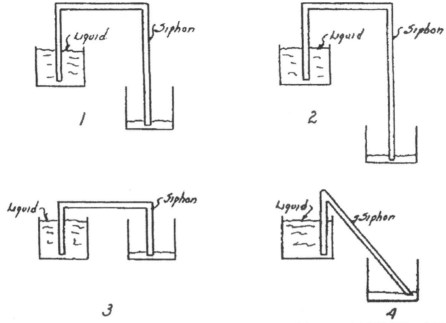

The *one* of the siphon arrangements shown above which would *MOST* quickly transfer a solution from the container on the left side to the one on the right side is numbered

    A. 1   B. 2   C. 3   D. 4

14. Static electricity is a hazard in industry CHIEFLY because it may cause

    A. dangerous or painful burns
    B. chemical decomposition of toxic elements
    C. sparks which can start an explosion
    D. overheating of electrical equipment

15.

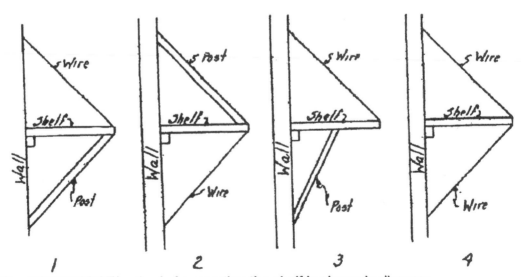

The *STRONGEST* method of supporting the shelf is shown in diagram

    A. 1   B. 2   C. 3   D. 4

13____

14____

15____

16. A row boat will float *deeper* in fresh water than in salt water *because*

    16____

    A. in the salt water the salt will occupy part of the space
    B. fresh water is heavier than salt water
    C. salt water is heavier than fresh water
    D. salt water offers less resistance than fresh water

17.

    17____

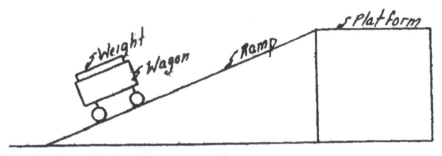

It is easier to get the load onto the platform by using the ramp than it is to lift it directly onto the platform. This is *true* because the effect of the ramp is to

    A. reduce the amount of friction so that less force is required
    B. distribute the weight over a larger area
    C. support part of the load so that less force is needed to move the wagon
    D. increase the effect of the moving weight

18.

    18____

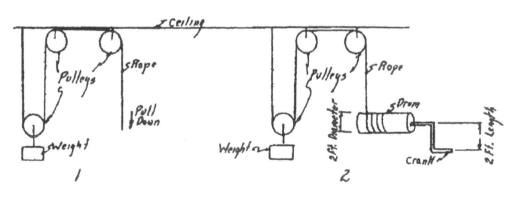

More weight can be lifted by the method shown in diagram 2 than as shown in diagram 1 because

    A. it takes less force to turn a crank than it does to pull in a straight line
    B. the drum will prevent the weight from falling by itself
    C. the length of the crank is larger than the radius of the drum
    D. the drum has more rope on it easing the pull

19.   19____

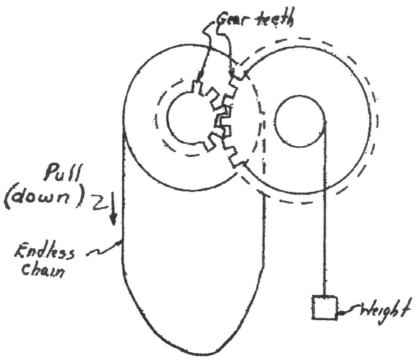

As the endless chain is pulled down in the direction shown, the weight will move

   A.   *up* faster than the endless chain is pulled down
   B.   *up* slower than the endless chain is pulled down
   C.   *down* faster than the endless chain is pulled down
   D.   *down* slower than the endless chain is pulled down

20.   Two balls of the same size, but different weights, are both dropped from a 10-ft. height.   20____
   The one of the following statements that is *MOST* accurate is that

   A.   both balls will reach the ground at the same time because they are the same size
   B.   both balls will reach the ground at the same time because the effect of gravity is
       the same on both balls
   C.   the heavier ball will reach the ground first because it weighs more
   D.   the lighter ball will reach the ground first because air resistance is greater on the
       heavier ball

21.   It is considered poor practice to increase the leverage of a wrench by placing a pipe over   21____
   the handle of the wrench. This is true *PRINCIPALLY* because

   A.   the wrench may break
   B.   the wrench may slip off the nut
   C.   it is harder to place the wrench on the nut
   D.   the wrench is more difficult to handle

22.

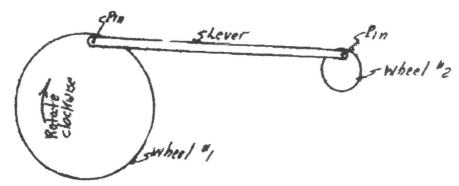

If wheel #1 is turned in the direction shown, wheel #2 will

- A. turn continously in a clockwise direction
- B. turn continously in a counterclockwise direction
- C. move back and fourth
- D. became jammed and both wheels will shop

23. ALL SOLID AREAS REPRESENT EQUAL WEIGHTS ATTACHED TO THE FLYWHEEL

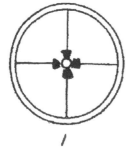
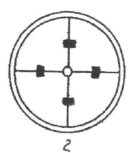

1   2   3

The above diagrams are of flywheels made of the same material with the same dimensions and attached to similar engines. The solid areas represent equal weights attached to the fly wheel. If all three engines are running at the same speed for the same length of time and the power to the engines is shut of simultaneously,

- A. wheel 1 will continue turning longest
- B. wheel 2 will continue turning longest
- C. wheel 3 will continue turning longest
- D. all three wheels will continue turning for the same time

24. The one of the following substance which expands when freezing is

    A. alcohol   B. ammonia   C. mercury   D. water

25. A piece of copper wire 30 feet long is cut into two pieces, 20 feet and 10 feet. The resistance of the *longer* piece, compared to the shorter, is

- A. one-half as much
- B. two-thirds as much
- C. one and one-half as much
- D. twice as much

KEY (CORRECT ANSWERS)

1.	C	11.	B
2.	A	12.	C
3.	B	13.	B
4.	D	14.	C
5.	B	15.	A
6.	D	16.	C
7.	B	17.	C
8.	D	18.	C
9.	B	19.	D
10.	B	20.	B

21.	A
22.	D
23.	C
24.	D
25.	D

———

TEST 2

DIRECTIONS: Each question or incomplete statement below is followed by several suggested answers or completions. Select the *one* that *BEST* answers the question or completes the statement. *PRINT THE LETTER OF THE CORRECT ANSWER IN THE SPACE AT THE RIGHT.*

Questions 1-2.

DIRECTIONS: Questions 1 and 2 are to be answered in accordance with the information in the following statement:

The electrical resistance of copper wires varies directly with their lengths and inversely with their cross section areas.

1. A piece of copper wire 30 feet long is cut into two pieces, 20 feet and 10 feet. The resistance of the *longer* piece, compared to the shorter, is   1____

   A. one-half as much
   B. two-thirds as much
   C. one and one-half as much
   D. twice as much

2. Two pieces of copper wire are each 10 feet long but the cross section area of one is 2/3 that of the other. The resistance of the piece with the *larger* cross-section area is   2____

   A. one-half the resistance of the smaller
   B. two-thirds the resistance of the smaller
   C. one and one-half times the resistance of the smaller
   D. twice the resistance of the smaller

3.   3____

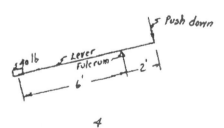

The arrangement of the lever which would require the *LEAST* amount of force to move the weight is shown in the diagram numbered

   A. 1   B. 2   C. 3   D. 4

4. Steel supporting beams in buildings often are surrounded by a thin layer of concrete to keep the beams from becoming hot and collapsing during a fire.   4____
   The *one* of the following statements which *BEST* explains how collapse is prevented by this arrangement is that concrete

   A. becomes stronger as its temperature is increased

    B.   acts as an insulating material
    C.   protects the beam from rust and corrosion
    D.   reacts chemically with steel at high temperatures

5.   If boiling water is poured into a drinking glass, the glass is likely to crack. If, however, a   5____
metal spoon first is placed in the glass, it is much less likely to crack. The reason that the
glass with the spoon is *less likely* to crack is that the spoon

    A.   distributes the water over a larger surface of the glass
    B.   quickly absorbs heat from the water
    C.   reinforces the glass
    D.   reduces the amount of water which can be poured into the glass

6.   It takes *more* energy to force water through a *long* pipe than through a *short* pipe of the   6____
same diameter. The *PRINCIPAL* reason for this is

    A. gravity   B. friction   C. inertia   D. cohesion

7.   A pump, discharging at 300 lbs.-per-sq.-inch pressure, delivers water through 100 feet   7____
of pipe laid horizontally. If the valve at the end of the pipe is shut so that no water can
flow, then the pressure at the valve is, for practical purposes,

    A.   *greater* than the pressure at the pump
    B.   *equal to* the pressure at the pump
    C.   *less* than the pressure at the pump
    D.   *greater or less* than the pressure at the pump, depending on the type of pump used

8.   The explosive force of a gas when stored under various pressures is given in the follow-   8____
ing table:

Storage Pressure	Explosive Force
10	1
20	8
30	27
40	64
50	125

The *one* of the following statements which *BEST* expresses the relationship between the
storage pressure and explosive force is that
    A.   there is no systematic relationship between an increase in storage pressure and
         an increase in explosive force
    B.   the explosive force varies as the square of the pressure
    C.   the explosive force varies as the cube of the pressure
    D.   the explosive force varies as the fourth power of the pressure

9.

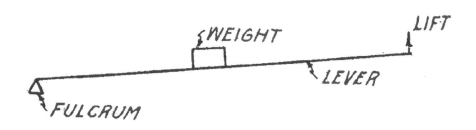

The leverage system in the sketch above is used to raise a weight. In order to *reduce* the amount of force required to raise the weight, it is necessary to

    A. decrease the length of the lever
    B. place the weight closer to the fulcrum
    C. move the weight closer to the person applying the force
    D. move the fulcrum further from the weight

10. In the accompanying sketch of a block and fall, if the end of the rope P is pulled so that it moves one foot, the distance the weight will be *raised* is

    A. 1/2 ft.
    B. 1 ft.
    C. 1 1/2 ft.
    D. 2 ft.

9 _____

10 _____

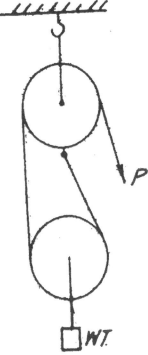

11.

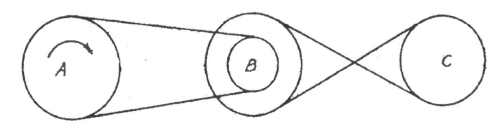

The above sketch diagrammatically shows a pulley and belt system. If pulley A is made to rotate in a clockwise direction, *then* pulley C will rotate

A. faster than pulley A and in a clockwise direction
B. slower than pulley A and in a clockwise direction
C. faster than pulley A and in a counter-clockwise direction
D. slower than pulley A and in a counter-clockwise direction

12.

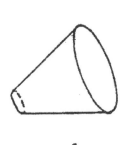

1   2   3   4

The above diagrams show four positions of the same object. The position in which this object is *MOST* stable is

A. 1   B. 2   C. 3   D. 4

13. The accompanying sketch diagrammatically shows a system of
meshing gears with relative diam-
eters as drawn. If gear 1 is made
to rotate in the direction of the
arrow, *then* the gear that will turn
FASTEST is numbered

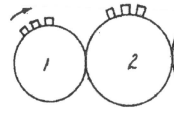

A. 1   B. 2   C. 3   D. 4

14.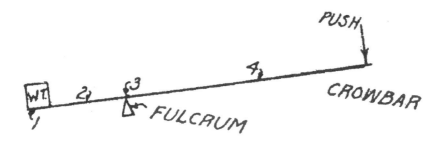

14____

The above sketch shows a weight being lifted by means of a crowbar.
The point at which the tendency for the bar to break is GREATEST is

A. 1   B. 2   C. 3   D. 4

15.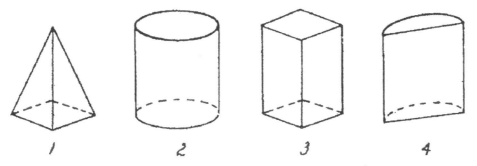

15____

The above sketches show four objects which weigh the same but have different shapes.
The object which is MOST difficult to tip over is numbered

A. 1   B. 2   C. 3   D. 4

16.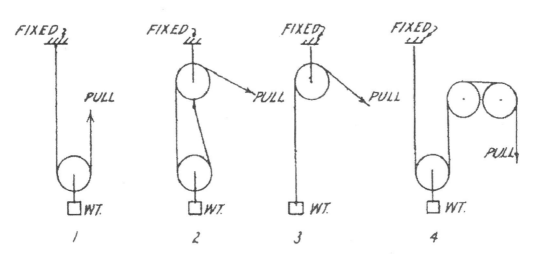

16____

An object is to be lifted by means of a system of lines and pulleys. Of the systems shown above, the one which would require the GREATEST force to be used in lifting the weight is the one numbered

A. 1   B. 2   C. 3   D. 4

147

17. An intense fire develops in a room in which carbon dioxide cylinders are stored. The
    PRINCIPAL hazard in this situation is that   17____

    A. the CO_2 may catch fire
    B. toxic fumes may be released
    C. the cylinders may explode
    D. released CO_2 may intensify the fire

18. At a fire involving the roof of a 5-story building, the firemen trained their hose stream on   18____
    the fire from a vacant lot across the street, aiming the stream at a point about 15 feet
    above the roof.
    In this situation, water in the stream would be traveling at the *GREATEST* speed

    A. as it leaves the hose nozzle
    B. at a point midway between the ground and the roof
    C. at the maximum height of the stream
    D. as it drops on the roof

19. A principle of lighting is that the intensity of illumination at a point is inversely proportional   19____
    to the square of the distance from the source of illumination.
    Assume that a pulley lamp is lowered from a position of 6 feet to one of three feet
    above a desk. According to the above principle, we would expect that the amount of
    illumination reaching the desk from the lamp in the lower position, as compared to the
    higher position, will be

    A. half as much   B. twice as much
    C. four times as much   D. nine times as much

20.   20____

         1   *2*   *3*   *4*

When standpipes are required in a structure, sufficient risers must be installed so that
no point on the floor is more than 120 feet from a riser.
The one of the above diagrams which gives the *MAXIMUM* area which can be covered
by one riser is

    A. 1   B. 2   C. 3   D. 4

21. Spontaneous combustion may be the reason for a pile of oily rags catching fire.   21____
    In general, spontaneous combustion is the *DIRECT* result of

    A. application of flame   B. falling sparks
    C. intense sunlight   D. chemical action
    E. radioactivity

22. In general, firemen are advised not to direct a solid stream of water on fires burning in electrical equipment. Of the following, the *MOST* logical reason for this instruction is that   22____

    A. water is a conductor of electricity
    B. water will do more damage to the electrical equipment than the fire
    C. hydrogen in water may explode when it comes in contact with electric current
    D. water will not effectively extinguish fires in electrical equipment
    E. water may spread the fire to other circuits

23. The height at which a fireboat will float in still water is determined *CHIEFLY* by the   23____

    A. weight of the water displaced by the boat
    B. horsepower of the boat's engines
    C. number of propellers on the boat
    D. curve the bow has above the water line
    E. skill with which the boat is maneuvered

24. When firemen are working at the nozzle of a hose they usually lean forward on the hose. The *most likely* reason for taking this position is that   24____

    A. the surrounding air is cooled, making the firemen more comfortable
    B. a backward force is developed which must be counteracted
    C. the firemen can better see where the stream strikes
    D. the fireman are better protected from injury by falling debris
    E. the stream is projected further

25. In general, the color and odor of smoke will *BEST* indicate   25____

    A. the cause of the fire
    B. the extent of the fire
    C. how long the fire has been burning
    D. the kind of material on fire
    E. the exact seat of the fire

—————

KEY (CORRECT ANSWERS)

1.	D	11.	C
2.	B	12.	A
3.	A	13.	D
4.	B	14.	C
5.	B	15.	A
6.	B	16.	C
7.	B	17.	C
8.	C	18.	A
9.	B	19.	C
10.	A	20.	C

21. D
22. A
23. A
24. B
25. D

TEST 3

DIRECTIONS : Each question or incomplete statement below is followed by several suggested answers or completions. Select the *one* that *BEST* answers the question or completes the statement. *PRINT THE LETTER OF THE CORRECT ANSWER IN THE SPACE AT THE RIGHT.*

1. As a demonstration, firemen set up two hose lines identical in every respect except that one was longer than the other. Water was then delivered through these lines from one pump and it was seen that the stream from the longer hose line had a shorter "throw," Of the following, the *MOST* valid explanation of this difference in "throw" is that the

    1____

   A. air resistance to the water stream is proportional to the length of hose
   B. time required for water to travel through the longer hose is greater than for the shorter one
   C. loss due to friction is greater in the longer hose than in the shorter one
   D. rise of temperature is greater in the longer hose than in the shorter one
   E. longer hose line probably developed a leak at one of the coupling joints

2. Of the following toxic gases, the *one* which is *MOST* dangerous because it cannot be seen and has no odor, is

    2____

   A. ether   B. carbon monoxide   C. chlorine
   D. ammonia   E. cooking gas

3. You are visiting with some friends when their young son rushes into the room with his clothes on fire. You immediately wrap him in a rug and roll him on the floor. The *MOST* important reason for your action is that the

    3____

   A. flames are confined within the rug
   B. air supply to the fire is reduced
   C. burns sustained will be third degree, rather than first degree
   D. whirling action will put out the fire
   E. boy will not suffer from shock

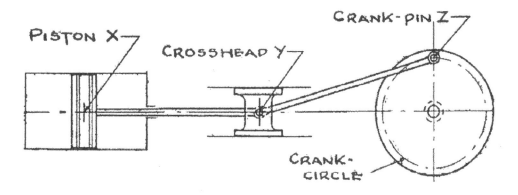

FIGURE I

Questions 4-6,

DIRECTIONS: The device shown in Figure I above represents schematically a mechanism commonly used to change reciprocating (back and forth) motion to rotation (circular) motion.
The following questions, numbered 4 to 6 inclusive, are to be answered with reference to this device.

4. Assume that piston X is placed in its extreme left position so that X, Y and Z are in a horizontal line. If a horizontal force to the right is applied to the piston X, we may then expect that

    A. the crank-pin Z will revolve clockwise
    B. the crosshead Y will move in a direction opposite to that of X
    C. the crank-pin Z will revolve counterclockwise
    D. no movement will take place
    E. the crank-pin Z will oscillate back and forth

4____

5. If we start from the position shown in the above diagram, and move piston X to the right, the result will be that

    A. the crank-pin Z will revolve counterclockwise and cross-head Y will move to the left
    B. the crank-pin Z will revolve clockwise and crosshead Y will move to the left
    C. the crank-pin Z will revolve clockwise and crosshead Y will move to the right
    D. the crank-pin Z will revolve clockwise and crosshead Y will move to the right
    E. crosshead Y will move to the left as piston X moves to the right

5____

6. If crank-pin Z is moved closer to the center of the crank circle, then the length of the

    A. stroke of piston X is increased
    B. stroke of piston X is decreased
    C. stroke of piston X is unchanged
    D. rod between the piston X and crosshead Y is increased
    E. rod between the piston X and crosshead Y is decreased

6____

Questions 7-8.

DIRECTIONS: Figure II represents schematically a block-and-fall tackle. The advantage derived from this machine is that the effect of the applied force is multiplied by the number of lines of rope directly supporting the load. The following two questions, numbered 7 and 8, are to be answered with reference to this figure.

7. Pull P is exerted on line T to raise the load L. The line in which the *LARGEST* strain is finally induced is line

    A. T   B. U   C. V   D. X   E. Y

7____

8. If the largest pull P that two men can apply to line T is 280 lbs., the *MAXIMUM* load L that they can raise without regard to frictional losses is, *most nearly,* _____ lbs.

    A. 1960
    B. 1680
    C. 1400
    D. 1260
    E. 1120

8_____

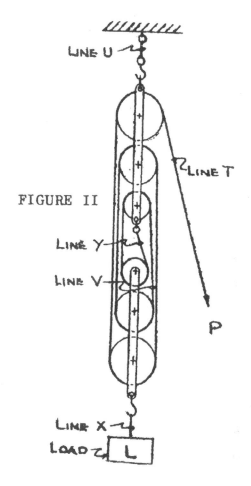

FIGURE II

Questions 9-13.

DIRECTIONS: Answer Questions 9 to 13 on the basis of Figure III. The diagram schematically illustrates part of a water tank. 1 and 5 are outlet and inlet pipes, respectively. 2 is a valve which can be used to open and close the outlet pipe by hand. 3 is a float which is rigidly connected to valve 4 by an iron bar, thus causing that valve to open or shut as the float rises or falls 4 is a hinged valve which controls the flow of water into the tank.

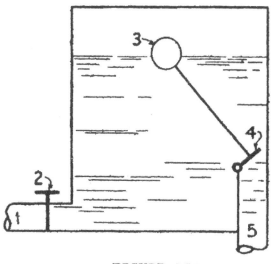

FIGURE III

9. If the tank is half filled and water is going out of pipe 1 more rapidly than it is coming in through pipe 5, *then*   9___

    A. valve 2 is closed
    B. float 3 is rising in the tank
    C. valve 4 is opening wider
    D. valve 4 is closed
    E. float 3 is stationary

10. If the tank is half filled with water and water is coming in through inlet pipe 5 more rapidly than it is going out through outlet pipe 1, *then*   10___

    A. valve 2 is closed
    B. float 3 is rising in the tank
    C. valve 4 is opening wider
    D. valve 4 is closed
    E. float 3 is stationary

11. If the tank is empty, then it can *normally* be expected that   11___

    A. float 3 is at its highest position
    B. float 3 is at its lowest position
    C. valve 2 is closed
    D. valve 4 is closed
    E. water will not come into the tank

12. If float 3 develops a leak, *then*   12___

    A. the tank will tend to empty
    B. water will tend to stop coming into the tank
    C. valve 4 will tend to close
    D. valve 2 will tend to close
    E. valve 4 will tend to remain open

13. Without any other changes being made, if the bar joining the float to valve 4 is removed and a slightly shorter bar substituted, *then*   13___

    A. a smaller quantity of water in the tank will be required before the float closes valve 4
    B. valve 4 will not open
    C. valve 4 will not close
    D. it is not possible to determine what will happen
    E. a greater quantity of water in the tank will be required before the float closes valve 4

Questions 14-18.

DIRECTIONS: Answer Questions 14 to 18 on the basis of Figure IV. A, B, C and D are four meshed gears forming a gear train. Gear A is the driver. Gears A and D each have twice as many teeth as gear B, and gear C has four times as many teeth as gear B. The diagram is schematic: the teeth go all around each gear.

14. *Two* gears which turn in the *same* direction are: 14_

    A. A and B
    B. B and C
    C. C and D
    D. D and A
    E. B and D

15. The *two* gears which revolve at the *same* speed are gears

15____

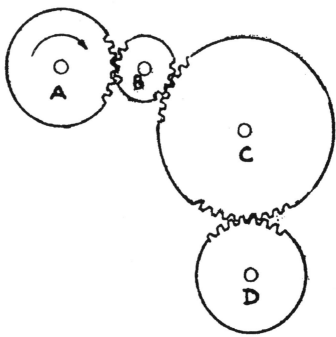

FIGURE IV

   A. A and C   B. A and D   C. B and C
   D. B and D   E. D and C

16. If all the teeth on gear C are stripped without affecting the teeth on gears A, B, and D, then rotation would occur *only* in gear(s)

16____

   A. C   B. D   C. A and B
   D. A, B, and D   E. B and D

17. If gear D is rotating at the rate of 100 RPM, then gear B is rotating at the rate of _____ RPM.

17____

   A. 25   B. 50   C. 100   D. 200   E. 400

18. If gear A turns at the rate of two revolutions per second, then the number of revolutions per second that gear C turns is

18____

   A. 1   B. 2   C. 3   D. 4   E. 8

Questions 19-23.

DIRECTIONS: Answer Questions 19 to 23 on the basis of Figure V. The diagram shows a water pump in cross section: 1 is a check valve, 2 and 3 are the spring and diaphragm, respectively, of the discharge valve, 4 is the pump piston; 5 is the inlet valve, and 6 is the pump cylinder. All valves permit the flow of water in one direction only.

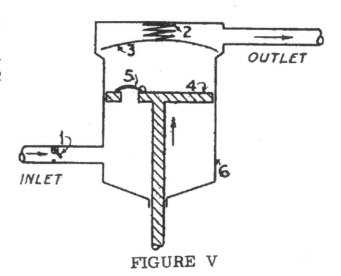

FIGURE V

19. When water is flowing through the outlet pipe,   19____

    A. check valve 1 is closed   B. diaphragm 3 is closed
    C. valve 5 is closed   D. spring 2 is fully extended
    E. the piston is on the downstroke

20. If valve 5 does not work properly and stays closed, *then*   20____

    A. the piston cannot move down   B. the piston cannot move up
    C. diaphragm 3 cannot open   D. check valve 1 cannot close
    E. the flow of water will be reversed

21. If diaphragm 3 does not work properly and stays in the open position, *then*   21____

    A. check valve 1 will not open
    B. valve 5 will not open
    C. spring 2 will be compressed
    D. spring 2 will be extended
    E. water will not flow through the inlet pipe

22. When valve 5 is open during normal operation of the pump, *then*   22____

    A. spring 2 is fully compressed
    B. the piston is on the upstroke
    C. water is flowing through check valve 1
    D. a vacuum is formed between the piston and the bottom of the cylinder
    E. diaphragm 3 is closed

23. If check valve 1 jams and stays closed, *then*   23____

    A. valve 5 will be open on both the upstroke and down stroke of the piston
    B. a vacuum will tend to form in the inlet pipe between the source of the water supply and check valve 1
    C. pressure on the cylinder side of check valve 1 will increase

D. less force will be required to move the piston down
E. more force will be required to move the piston down

24. The one of the following which *BEST* explains why smoke usually rises from a fire is that   24____

    A. cooler, heavier air displaces lighter, warm air
    B. heat energy of the fire propels the smoke upward
    C. suction from the upper air pulls the smoke upward
    D. burning matter is chemically changed into heat energy

25. The practice of racing a car engine to warm it up in cold weather, generally, is   25____

    A. *good, MAINLY* because repeated stalling of the engine and drain on the battery is avoided
    B. *bad, MAINLY* because too much gas is used to get the engine heated
    C. *good, MAINLY* because the engine becomes operational in the shortest period of time
    D. *bad, MAINLY* because proper lubrication is not established rapidly enough

---

KEY (CORRECT ANSWERS)

1.	C		11.	B
2.	B		12.	E
3.	B		13.	A
4.	D		14.	E
5.	D		15.	B
6.	B		16.	C
7.	B		17.	D
8.	B		18.	A
9.	C		19.	C
10.	B		20.	A

21.	C
22.	E
23.	D
24.	A
25.	D

Basic Fundamentals of Automotive Vehicles

Contents

Basic Fundamentals of Automotive Vehicles

This chapter provides general information on starting, operating, and maintaining automotive equipment for hauling materials, equipment, passengers, and fuels. It includes information on the capabilities, gross limits, and utilization of automotive equipment. Also covered are safety precautions to be observed when operating or working near automotive equipment, inflating and changing tires, and handling, loading, hauling, and offloading materials, equipment, and fuels. Knowledge of the information in this chapter and its application to the job will enable you to perform your duties more efficiently.

I. TYPES OF AUTOMOTIVE VEHICLES

PASSENGER CARRYING VEHICLES

The most common types of passenger carrying vehicles are automobiles, buses, carry-alls, station wagons, and ambulances. These vehicles are used to transport light cargo and personnel.

HAULING VEHICLES

The most common standard trucks are classified by weight-carrying capacity and by body type. The weight-carrying capacity may be referred to as light trucks, from 1/2 to 2 tons; medium trucks, from 1 1/2 to 2 1/2 tons; and heavy duty trucks, from 2 1/2 to 5 tons.

A body-type classification may refer to the principal purpose for which the truck is used (hauling of cargo), or to the physical character of the particular body (stake, van, or dump).

TRUCK-TRACTOR AND SEMITRAILER

Besides standard trucks, industry uses many truck-tractors with semitrailers. Truck-tractors used to tow semitrailers may be gasoline or diesel engine powered, and range in capacity from 5 tons through 15 tons. Semitrailers are made in a variety of body types such as personnel carrying, fuel tank, cargo van, stake, bitumen tank, and low-bed (equipment hauling). Low-bed trailers of several lengths and widths up to 75-ton capacity are also used.

FUEL HANDLING VEHICLES

Fuel handling vehicles are classified as *fuel tank trucks* or *fuel tank semitrailers*. Each vehicle has distinguishing characteristics (model, size, and capacity). The purpose of fuel handling vehicles is to load, haul, and discharge fuel to other vehicles, aircraft, or fuel depots.

II. WEIGHT DISTRIBUTION AND LOAD SECURING METHODS

Distribution of cargo has definite bearing on the life of tires, axles, frame, and other parts of the vehicles. The fact that a truck or trailer is not loaded beyond its gross vehicle weight capacity does not mean that the individual tires and axles may not be overloaded by faulty distribution of the cargo.

As an aid to properly loading a truck or semitrailer, the center of the payload must be determined. In a truck, the position of the center of payload is the center of the body, or the point midway between the rear of the driver's cab and the tailgate. In a truck-tractor semi-trailer unit, the position of the center of the payload is roughly the center of the semitrailer body, because the tractor's front wheels seldom carry any of the payload. When loading, it is important that the maximum capacity of the vehicle is not exceeded over any one of the axles and, if possible, that loads are distributed so that there is a less-than-maximum axle loading. No vehicle will be loaded over its rated capacity without direct authorization.

The trend of vehicle manufacturers is to rate trucks in terms of maximum gross vehicle weight instead of by tonnage capacities. This has resulted in poor utilization of trucks because of loading below rated capacities. It has also caused confusion, in many instances as to the maximum pounds of payload that may be transported in trucks rated in tonnage capacities.

The maximum permissible payload of a truck is determined by deducting the curb weight and weight of the driver (175 lbs.) from the manufacturer's gross vehicle weight rating. The maximum gross vehicle weight rating for a specified operating condition applies only when the tires and equipment on the truck are in accordance with the manufacturer's recommendations for the specified operating condition, which is referred to as *ideal, moderate,* or *severe,*

Ideal conditions mean that the truck is operated over improved, level roads, such as asphalt or concrete, at constant, relatively moderate speeds, with no adverse weather or road conditions. Under these conditions, recommended payload equals 100 percent of maximum permissible payload.

Moderate conditions mean that the truck is operated at high speeds over improved highways, such as asphalt or concrete, with or without long or steep grades, or at moderate speeds over semi-improved roads with gravel or equivalent surfacing, in gently rolling country with few steep grades and no adverse weather or road conditions. Under these conditions, recommended payload equals 80 percent of maximum permissible payload.

Severe conditions means that the vehicle is operated off the highway on rough or hilly terrain or over unimproved or pioneer access roads with deep ruts, holes, or steep grades; or where traffic has created deep holes or ruts in heavy snow covering normally good city streets or highways. Under these conditions, the recommended payload equals 64 percent of maximum permissible payload.

It is important that the payload weight be properly distributed over the body so that the percentage of weight carried by the front axle and that carried by the rear axle will be in the ratio for which the vehicle was designed.

A knowledge of the following terms will give you a better understanding of payload weight distribution for vehicles.

Gross Vehicle Weight (GVW) means the total weight of the loaded truck. It is the sum of the weights of the chassis, accessories, equipment attachments, cab, body, full complement of fuel, lubricants and coolant, payload, and driver.

Curb weight is the weight of the empty truck - without payload and driver - including fuel tank, cooling system, and crankcase filled. It also includes the weight of tools, spare wheel, and all other equipment specified as standard.

Dry chassis weight means the weight of the chassis complete with cowl, but not including weight of cab, body or fifth wheel, spare wheel, tire assembly with carrier, fuel, lubricants, coolant, tools, payload, operator, and frame reinforcement where required.

Payload allowance means the maximum weight of material that can be transported.

Check material for damage before and during the loading operation. Do not accept damaged material unless the damage is noted on the dispatch order or written acknowledgement of the damage is received from the supply department.

Physical dimensions, capacities, weight limitations, and load distribution of trucks and trailers vary greatly. These variations preclude the covering of all types of loads. Therefore, the methods and procedures described here must be considered typical.

There are conditions which can cause load movement while in transit. However, almost all load movement can be prevented by proper blocking and bracing. All loads must be balanced in the vehicle lengthwise and crosswise before the vehicle is operated. Precautions must be taken to prevent vertical movement because of sudden stops or travel over rough terrain as vertical movement can cause the breakdown of good blocking and bracing. If the load is not placed tightly or is out of alignment, the unbalanced loading will cause unequal pressures. The use of bulkheads, separation gates, dividers (lengthwise and crosswise), layer separations, runners, blocks, cleats, and strapping, properly fabricated and applied, will prevent most load movement.

The truck and trailer combination can be adapted to transport various types of materials such as fragile, bulky, compact, dense, and rough items, and high center of gravity items. In order to accommodate the variety of items you must plan the load, properly prepare the truck or trailer, and secure the load to the vehicle. This will prevent any possibility of the load shifting or falling off the vehicle, shifting and contacting other traffic, fouling underpasses, culverts, bridge abutments, and creating a hazard to pedestrians. Securing the load can be accomplished by staying the load with proper lines, or chains secured by tie-down or binders. Use appropriate gear such as paper, cloth, or other type filler to protect fragile items from damage by chafing (rubbing together).

If the truck or trailer is not enclosed or covered, use tarpaulins to cover the cargo and prevent exposure, damage, loss of cargo, or littering.

When transporting pipe, lumber, or other unusually long loads which extend beyond the truck body, attach a red flag to the end of the load and use a red light to mark the end of the load when traveling at night.

Before operating a truck or trailer loaded with unusually heavy, long, or odd-sized materials, ensure that the load weight and dimensions are within the prescribed state and local regulations. If oversize or overweight vehicles are required to be used for a particular job, obtain special permits prior to moving such loads or vehicles on public highways.

When transporting explosives or material interstate, adhere to all instructions, state and local laws, and I.C.C. regulations.

PRINCIPLES OF OPERATION OF PASSENGER CARRYING VEHICLES

You should have knowledge about how components are assembled to make up the automotive chassis consisting of the engine, frame, power train, wheels, steering and braking systems.

Passenger carrying vehicles which include automobiles, buses, carry-alls, station wagons, and ambulances are all similar in their principles of operation although some assemblies and components will be different in body styles, types, and sizes.

PRINCIPLES OF OPERATION OF HAULING VEHICLES

A typical dump truck is equipped with a dump body which has a struck capacity of 5 cubic yards, and is hinged to the rear of a subframe which is mounted directly on the truck chassis. The hoist assembly used to raise and lower the dump body is comprised of a pair of double-acting hydraulic cylinders, a positive-displacement gear-type hydraulic pump, a hydraulic oil reservoir, and connecting

high pressure-type hoses. The hydraulic pump is driven by a propeller shaft connected to the power-take-off. Operation of the hoist assembly is controlled by the dump body control lever located to the left of the driver's seat.

By disengaging the vehicle clutch and shifting the dump body control lever to either position other than neutral, the power-take-off and hoist pump engages. When moving the control lever to the power-up position and engaging the clutch, the dump body will raise (when the dump body reaches its limit of travel, it automatically stops). Upon moving the control lever to the power-down position, the dump body will lower. Moving the control lever to the neutral position and locking it will secure the dump body.

Another hauling vehicle used is the truck-tractor and semitrailer combination. This combination is unique in the manner in which the semitrailer and truck-tractor are attached to perform the hauling services for which they are intended. A large part of the weight of the semitrailer in this combination is supported by a connection, called the fifth wheel, the remaining weight is supported by the wheels of the semitrailer. The trailer braking system (usually air) is coupled to the towing vehicle by a flexible hose and a detachable coupling. The trailer braking system is usually designed so that it will keep the trailer in place when the couplings are disconnected. The trailer is also equipped with a landing gear which is a retractable support under the front end of the semitrailer. This gear is used to hold up the front end when it is uncoupled from the truck-tractor. When semitrailers are coupled and uncoupled, it is important that operation of the landing gear be coordinated with operation of the fifth wheel lock. If the landing gear is elevated before the fifth wheel connection is fully locked, the front end of the semitrailer will drop to the ground when the truck-tractor is driven away, with the possibility of damaging both the load and the semitrailer. Before the semitrailer is uncoupled, the brake couplings should be disconnected so that the semitrailer brakes are applied to prevent it from moving.

The method of connecting the truck-tractor to the semitrailer is by means of a fifth wheel. The upper fifth wheel plate is securely attached to the underside of the front end of the semi-trailer frame. Permanently attached to the center of the upper fifth wheel plate is a kingpin by which the truck-tractor pulls the semitrailer after the upper fifth wheel is attached to the truck-tractor lower fifth wheel. The kingpin is locked into position by a kingpin lock which is a ring on the lower fifth wheel that clamps around this kingpin. The kingpin lock is operated by a hand lever that extends to the side of the lower fifth wheel and can be released by pulling it out when the semitrailer is to become detached from the truck-tractor.

PRINCIPLES OF OPERATION OF FUEL HAULING VEHICLES

A typical <u>fuel tank</u> truck is equipped with a tank body divided into compartments. Each compartment has a manhole and filler cover assembly, bottom sump or well, discharge valves with screen assemblies and drainpipe. The drainpipes end in a manifold in the equipment compartment. The compartment also houses a delivery pump, a discharge valve control assembly, a pump delivery line gate valve, automatic dump valve drain tube valves, a gravity line gate valve, a filter separator, a pressure gate, a meter, a water separate chamber, and a grounding cable.

The delivery pump is powered by the transfer power takeoff, which is controlled by the transfer power shifting lever located in the driver's compartment. The lever is moved backward to the <u>engaged</u> position to engage the power takeoff which causes the pump to operate. The lever is moved forward to the <u>disengaged</u> position to disengage the power takeoff and stop the pump.

The discharge valve control operating levers control the discharge valves located at the bottom of each tank compartment. Pulling back on a lever opens a discharge valve and permits the flow of fuel into the piping system. Squeezing the trip rod operating handle mounted on the lever, and moving the lever forward, locks the compartment valve and shuts off the flow of fuel.

In an emergency, the discharge valve control remote control lever, located on the left side of the discharge valve control operating lever bank, provides a means of locking all discharge valves. Pulling the handle causes a release lever to trip the operating levers and locks the valves.

III. AUTOMOTIVE VEHICLE OPERATION

The sole source of complete and authentic information on operating a given automotive vehicle is the operator's manual issued by the manufacturer.

The information given in this section describes the prestart checks, starting checks, and operating procedures which are typical of automotive vehicles used.

PRESTART CHECKS

Before operating any vehicle, be sure that it is ready for the run. A prestart check should begin as you approach your vehicle. Take a look at it. Does its overall appearance seem normal? Oftentimes you will be able to tell from this first look if your vehicle has a broken spring or other exterior defects.

As you continue with the prestart check, move around to the front of your vehicle and raise the cap. If the coolant level is not visible, add coolant. Continual lowering of the level of coolant indicates a possible leak in the cooling system. In freezing weather, test the anti-freeze solution in the radiator with a hydrometer. If necessary, add enough antifreeze to the coolant to prevent freezing at predicted minimum temperatures. Be sure to report a leaking cooling system on the Operator's Trouble Report so that corrective action can be taken by the maintenance shop.

Next check the level of the lubricating oil in the crankcase. It should be at or near the full mark on the dipstick. If it is not, add sufficient oil to raise the level to full. If the oil is dirty and gritty when rubbed between the fingertips, it will have to be changed.

Fan belts should be checked for defects in the belt, and excessive looseness or tightness. When found to be defective, the belts must be replaced. When found to be too loose or too tight, adjust according to the manufacturer's specifications.

Battery water level must be checked. If the level is not visible, add battery water to the level required. Check for loose battery wire connections, and tighten if required. Have worn or frayed battery wires replaced by the maintenance shop.

Close the hood, making sure that it latches properly.

Check the fuel tank. Most fuel tank gages register when the ignition switch is turned on. If the fuel gage is not working properly, and you have no way of knowing how much fuel is in the tank, fill it up. Running out of fuel could be very inconvenient and embarassing. Be sure to report improper operation of the fuel gage on the Operator's Trouble Report, so that corrective action can be taken by the maintenance shop.

Leaks found during your checks can often be corrected by tightening bolts, filler plugs, and line connections. If these steps fail to stop a leak, report the trouble for corrective action by the maintenance shop.

As you check the wheels and tires, be sure the tire pressure is as recommended (usually stenciled on each fender of the vehicle) by using either a tire gage or a tire air-hose that is equipped with a gage. Be particularly alert for uneven tread wear; this condition may indicate misalignment, need for balancing, or improper inflation. You may replace the tire at the tire shop, but balancing or alignment will be handled by the maintenance shop. When inspecting the wheels, see that the wheel flange bolts are in place and properly secured.

As you continue your prestart checks, examine the vehicle body for missing components, dents, doors that close improperly, and door windows and windshield glass that are cracked or broken. Next look under the vehicle to check the drive shaft, rear end, and rear axles for leaks or other obvious defects. Any discrepancies must be reported on the Operator's Trouble Report, so that corrective action can be taken by the maintenance shop.

When you have completed the external portion of the prestart checks, get into the cab and check the lights by turning on the light switch and observing whether the headlights are burning on both high and low beam. Have someone observe whether the stoplights on the rear of the vehicle go on when you apply the brakes. As you inspect the lights, wipe the glass lenses with a cloth. A film of mud or dust can cut light beams considerably. If the vehicle has special lights, such as turn signals, fog lights, and spotlights, they, too, must be in good working condition. Test the horn, check seat belts, and inspect the rear view mirror for damage. Before moving on, check the condition of the windshield wiper blades. In addition, check the vehicle's brakes, making sure that the brake lines are not broken or leaking, and that the parking brake cable and assembly are in working order. If any item needs to be adjusted, repaired, or replaced, note the trouble on the Operator's Trouble Report, so that corrective action can be performed by the maintenance shop.

A prestart check will be slightly different for each type vehicle, but the basic principles apply to all. At first, these checks may seem like a long and useless procedure. Once you have established a routine, however, you will find that the complete check requires only a few minutes. Many times this check will save you hours of trouble in the field or on the road.

STARTING CHECKS BEFORE OPERATION

After starting the engine, but before putting the vehicle or equipment into motion, make a few additional checks. First, and most important, make certain that you get an oil pressure indication. This indication may be below operating range at first, but be certain that it is registering. If your equipment has an oil pressure low warning light, make certain the light does not remain on more than several seconds after the engine is started. If the light does not go out after several seconds of engine operation, stop the engine and call a mechanic. Occasionally, a defective system causes the light to stay on, but in either case you will need the mechanic.

Your vehicle or equipment ammeter should also register a positive charge as the engine starts to run. This may be indicated by an ammeter which begins to register in a positive direction or by a red light which goes out when the charging begins. You should also check the temperature indicator, which should start to move upward on its scales as the engine warms up. In addition, check the windshield wipers to see if they are operating properly.

DURING OPERATIONS CHECKS

When a vehicle or piece of equipment is not operating properly, there are various symptoms by which the malfunction can be identified. You should be able to recognize these symptoms immediately and stop the machine before damage results. We have already mentioned the starting checks for oil pressure and the electrical system. Now let's look at some of the troubles that may occur during operation.

Temperature. The operating temperature of your piece of equipment is a measure of its mechanical condition. An engine that is running too hot or too cold is not functioning properly, and the cause of the high or low temperature should be determined immediately. If there is trouble in the cooling system, the engine, in most cases, will overheat.

Before you run your piece of equipment into the repair shop or call a mechanic, make a few checks to see if you can locate the trouble. First, check the radiator. If the water is low, refill. In addition, check to see if there are leaves or other matter clogging air passages of the radiator grill. Check the oil level. An insufficient amount of oil can cause overheating. Loose, slipping water pump belts and fan belts will cause overheating; check and tighten them if they are slipping.

If you eliminate these possible causes of overheating, and the temperature is still not normal, it is time to call a mechanic.

Oil Pressure. As mentioned earlier, you should make certain that oil pressure registers when the engine is started. High pressure readings may be observed while the engine is warming up in cold weather, before the oil has reached operating temperature. After a brief warmup period, the gage indicator should return to normal. Do not forget, however, to keep constant check on oil pressure throughout the day. If the pressure should drop, stop the engine and notify a mechanic.

There are a number of things that can cause low oil pressure. Diluted lubricating oil will cause a drop in pressure. If the oil is at the proper level, but is thin and lacks body, it may have been diluted with fuel leaking past the piston rings. The crankcase should be drained and refilled with the proper grade of oil. If frequent oil dilution or low oil pressure continues after changing the oil, your engine needs further services of a mechanic. As mentioned before, on rare occasions the trouble will be in the pressure gage rather than in the engine proper.

Electrical System. If your piece of equipment has a generator and battery, the ammeter indicates the condition of the electrical system. If the ammeter shows a discharge when the engine is running and all electrical accessories such as lights have been turned off, there is something wrong with the system; call a mechanic. Some vehicles have a warning light instead of an ammeter; if this light comes on and stays on during engine operation (except when the engine is idling), this too is an indication of trouble in the electrical system.

Smoking. Whenever you are operating motorized equipment and you see smoke coming from the exhaust pipe, there is trouble of some sort. The most common causes of smoking in a gasoline engine are worn pistons, rings, or cylinders, and faulty fuel mixtures. Smoking caused by worn engine parts is usually coupled with high oil consumption and calls for a major overhaul.

There are a number of mechanical troubles that will cause a diesel to smoke. If the engine is running too cool, the exhaust will form a cloud of white smoke. If the radiator is equipped with adjustable shutters, close them until the engine reaches the proper operating temperature. If the engine does not have shutters, place a partial covering over the radiator to bring the temperature up. Another cause of smoky exhaust is a clogged air cleaner. Follow the maintenance instructions printed on the air cleaner.

If the engine is allowed to idle for considerable periods, there will be more fuel injected into the cylinder than will burn, and consequently it will smoke. Do not idle the engine for long periods.

If the engine is subjected to loads that cause it to slow or lug down, it will begin to smoke. The remedy is to keep the engine revved up and to use the proper gear to handle the load. If you eliminate these causes of smoking and the engine still smokes, it is probably due to injectors, valves, fuel pumps, or worn piston rings; any of these conditions means a repair job for the mechanics.

Wheel Trouble. If you are operating automotive equipment, your hands on the steering wheel will tell you if the vehicle pulls to the right or to the left. You will feel vibrations caused by unbalanced wheels. When you apply the brakes, you will be able to feel whether the wheel is pulled to the right or to the left; thus you will know whether the front wheel brakes are operating evenly.

When you feel the vehicle pull to one side, stop and check the tires. If the tires are evenly inflated and the vehicle still pulls to one side, you should have the wheel alignment and the wheels checked by a mechanic. Your hands on the wheel will also tell you if the vehicle turns hard and whether the play in the steering wheel is excessive.

Transmission and Differential. Transmission difficulties may be characterized by shifting difficulty, gears jamming, and by unusual noises from the area where the transmission is located. This is true of a vehicle having either a manual or an automatic transmission. About the only thing that an equipment operator can do is to check the level of lubricant; if the transmission is low on lubricant, fill it to the proper level.

Differential trouble can often be recognized by noise from the differential area. However, noise from defective universal joints, rear wheel bearings, tires, or mufflers are sometimes mistaken for differential trouble. Stop the vehicle if noise occurs. For the purpose of operational maintenance with respect to differentials, an equipment operator has the responsibility of seeing that lubricant is at the proper level and bringing it up to the proper level if it is low. If there is differential trouble and you find that the level is not low, you should turn the job of locating and correcting the trouble over to a mechanic.

Brake Troubles. If your equipment is fitted with airbrakes, be aware of the air pressure indicator reading at all times. The reading may be too high; a high reading would probably indicate a faulty gage, a governor out of adjustment, or a defective governor. The most usual trouble with airbrakes is too little pressure. Low pressure can indicate a number of things, but most commonly it indicates a defective air safety valve, a governor out of adjustment, or an excessively worn compressor.

The air pressure gage is only one of the possible means by which you will discover trouble. Some of the other airbrake troubles are that they release too slowly, grab, or brake unevenly.

On hydraulic brakes, a soft, spongy pedal indicates either improper adjustment of air in the system. A pedal that goes to, or nearly to, the floorboard calls for immediate attention by a mechanic. Stops that require excessive pressure on the pedal, and brakes that are overly sensitive and grab when only slight pressure is applied to the pedal are other troubles that mean work for the mechanic.

Be sure that your brakes are in the best possible condition; your life may depend on them.

Clutches. If the clutch does not completely disengage when the pedal is entirely depressed, or if the clutch takes hold too near the floorboard, you should report the condition to a mechanic.

Vibration. On most of the equipment you operate, you will feel a certain amount of vibration; an unusual amount of vibration should not have to shake you out of your seat to make you realize that something is wrong. Unbalanced wheels, a cylinder that is not firing, a bent drive shaft, and other mechanical defects will cause excessive vibration.

After operating a piece of equipment for a period of time, you should be so aware of its characteristic sounds and its feel that you will be able to detect the slightest variation from normal operation. You may not be able to diagnose the mechanical symptoms, but you should be able to recognize trouble when it starts.

OPERATING PASSENGER CARRYING AND HAULING VEHICLES

After completing all prestarting and starting checks, and ensuring everything is in order, place the transmission in <u>neutral</u> or <u>park</u> and start the engine. Before you pull onto the road, be sure that it is clear enough for you to do so safely.

If your vehicle has an automatic transmission, set the transmission lever at D (Drive) or push in the D button. Release the emergency brake and speed up the engine by depressing the accelerator about one quarter of the way toward the floorboard. The vehicle should accelerate in <u>Low</u> smoothly. At a speed of about 18 to 25 mph under normal acceleration, the transmission should shift automatically into Drive. On some vehicles you must release the accelerator momentarily to let the transmission shift into Drive. A faint click in the transmission indicates the shift to the higher gear.

With a standard transmission, depress the clutch pedal, shift into first (low) gear, release the emergency brake, and engage the clutch slowly and smoothly while speeding up the engine a bit with the accelerator. Let the vehicle get up to about 10 to 15 mph before shifting into second gear, and to about 20 to 25 mph before shifting into third or high gear. Depress the clutch pedal before each shift, and release it smoothly after shifting.

On many vehicles with standard transmission, the gear shift lever is mounted on the steering column. Refer to the vehicle instruction manual for gear shifting directions.

<u>Up and Down Grade.</u> In starting a vehicle with a standard transmission up a grade from a stationary position, keep the emergency brake on to prevent the vehicle from rolling backward. Push in the clutch, shift into low, then ease off on the clutch pedal. As the clutch begins to take hold, release the emergency brake slowly, <u>at the same time,</u> increasing the speed of the engine. If these operations are performed carefully, the vehicle should start smoothly. Shift the vehicle into second only when it has reached enough speed to continue upgrade without laboring or jerking. You may not be able to shift from second to high until the end of the grade. If the grade is very steep, you may have to use low gear all the way up.

Downgrade always use the same gear that would be used going upgrade. Depress the clutch, shift into neutral, accelerate the engine to a speed that will pull the vehicle in a lower gear, then shift into the lower gear. If the procedure is efficiently carried out, the shift will be virtually noiseless.

UNDER NO CIRCUMSTANCES SHOULD THE VEHICLE COAST DOWNGRADE IN NEUTRAL. A vehicle out of gear is out of control except, possibly, when the brakes are applied. Even then the vehicle may pick up speed in excess of its braking ability, and you risk not only burning up the brakes, but having a serious accident as well.

<u>Low Range and Double-Clutching.</u> Heavy trucks may be equipped also with a two-speed rear axle and have what is known as a <u>low range.</u> By shifting to this low range, you tap the extra engine power that is needed to start an extremely heavy load, in rough driving, and in steep climbing. Under normal driving conditions, you would use the normal range.

No matter what kind of load the truck is carrying, start out in low gear, not in second. Together, the low range and low gear give maximum starting power. Take your time and accelerate smoothly in each gear before shifting to the next higher gear. Under some road or load conditions, the series of shifts from low to high may require as much as a mile of travel.

The transmissions of some trucks and buses are constructed in a form which makes it necessary to <u>double-clutch</u> to prevent the clashing and grinding of gears when shifting. Double-clutching adjusts engine speed to vehicle speed in a particular gear.

Double-clutching requires some practice. If you can possibly arrange to do so, take a truck around a given area with a supervisor or other experienced equipment operator to instruct you.

```
DOUBLE-CLUTCHING FROM A LOWER
      TO A HIGHER GEAR

  • Push in clutch pedal
    • Take foot off gas pedal
      • Shift into neutral
        • Let out clutch pedal
          • Wait momentarily
            • Push in clutch pedal again
          • Shift to higher gear
        • Let out clutch pedal
      • Depress gas pedal
```

```
DOUBLE-CLUTCHING FROM A HIGHER
      TO A LOWER GEAR

  • Push in clutch pedal
    • Take foot off gas pedal
      • Shift into neutral
        • Let out clutch pedal
          • Accelerate engine
            • Push in clutch pedal again
          • Shift to lower gear
        • Let out clutch pedal
      • Depress gas pedal
```

<u>Steering.</u> Proper steering is a matter of keeping your hands on the wheel, your eyes on the road, and your mind on safe driving. It also means keeping the vehicle on your side of the road, avoiding holes and obstructions, and passing other vehicles safely.

If your vehicle steers hard, pulls to the right or left, or the front wheels shimmy, try to find the cause of the trouble at once. It may be due to nothing more than underinflated tires, or it may be caused by the wheels being out of balance or alignment. It may also mean that some part of the steering mechanism needs adjusting, or repair.

If not accustomed to power steering, you may have difficulty at first in guiding this type of vehicle, because its steering mechanism responds more readily than one with conventional steering. Under power steering, a mere finger nudge of the steering wheel will turn the vehicle from its path.

<u>Backing.</u> Not all driving is forward. You will also have to back into loading platforms and parking spaces and into position lor shovel loading and other jobs on construction projects. Backing must be done with skill and caution. If the rear view of your vehicle is restricted, have someone direct you. Otherwise, get out frequently to check whether the way is clear. NOTE: The operator is responsible for all backing accidents.

<u>Curves.</u> Speeding under any conditions is dangerous and unsafe, but speeding on curves is extremely dangerous for at least four reasons: it increases the hazard of skidding; it heightens the _ possibility of load shifting; it wears tires away very fast; and the vehicle may run off the road or overturn.

It is not easy to state at what speed you can safely round a curve. The maximum safe speed depends on the arc of the curve, the width of the road, and the condition of its surface. Many curves are posted with safe speed limit signs, but on many, YOU still must judge how fast to take them.

In approaching a curve, SLOW DOWN as soon as it comes into view, then accelerate enough to keep the vehicle pulling steadily. If the road ahead curves frequently, maintain a speed moderate enough to keep the vehicle on an even keel, using the highest gear possible. Avoid using the brakes. NEVER try to pass another vehicle on a curve. Stay on your own side of the center line.

Skids. To avoid skids, watch for obstructions, pavement breaks, holes, shoulder edges, and loose gravel that might grab your wheels. Beware of wet roads, roads strewn with leaves, roads full of mud or slush, and railroad and trolley tracks.

To prevent going into a skid, cut down your speed, and increase the distance between your vehicle and the one ahead. Do not accelerate too fast or the wheels may spin; drive in as high a gear as possible. The higher the gear, the less the tendency to skid. Should you get into a skid, however, turn the wheels IN THE DIRECTION OF THE SKID, stay in gear with the clutch engaged, and accelerate slightly to help straighten the course of the vehicle. DO NOT APPLY THE BRAKES; you will only increase the skid by locking the wheels. If any slowing is necessary, it should be done in a lower gear.

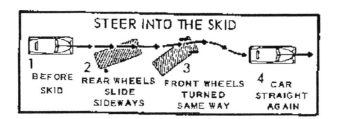

Off and On The Shoulder. Getting off and on the shoulder is a common occurrence on narrow roads and in congested traffic, and it usually is not difficult to get back on the road. However, if the shoulder is lower than the road, first change to a lower gear without braking. Second, instead of scrapping or tearing away the side walls of your tires by trying to creep back upon the road gradually, proceed slowly until you are able to get back by making a sharp angle turn to the left.

OPERATING TRUCK TRACTOR AND SEMITRAILER

Before setting out with a truck tractor and semitrailer, you must know the procedures for coupling and uncoupling the truck tractor from the semitrailer. To couple the truck tractor to the semitrailer, proceed as follows:

1. Place wheel chocks in front of and behind the trailer wheels.

2. Make sure the fifth wheel lock is open; then back the tractor close enough to the trailer to permit coupling of the brake lines,

3. Connect the brake hoses in the proper order by first connecting the truck tractor <u>service</u> air line hose to the trailer, followed by the <u>emergency</u> air line hose.

4. Open the cutout valve to allow pressure to build up in the reserve tank on the trailer.

5. Apply pressure to the trailer brakes, if they are operated independently. If the trailer brakes are not operated independently, proceed as described below.

      a.   For vacuum-operated brakes, turn off the service line valve and disconnect the hose; this should automatically apply pressure to the trailer brakes.

      b.   For air-operated brakes, turn off the emergency line valve and disconnect the hose; this should automatically apply pressure to the trailer brakes.

6. Back the tractor under the trailer until the fifth wheel engages the trailer kingpin and locks. If the tractor is not in line to engage the trailer kingpin and must be repositioned, uncouple the airhose before moving the tractor to avoid breaking the hose.

7. When the fifth wheel and the kingpin are locked, test security of the hookup. Remove the chocks, place the tractor in first gear, engage the clutch, and move the tractor forward slightly while applying pressure to the brakes.

8. If the trailer is properly connected, stop the tractor and set the hand brake; double check all couplings, reconnect the air brake hose, and open the air valve.

9. Connect the trailer electrical power line; check for proper operation of lights and, where applicable, heating or refrigeration equipment.

10. Raise the trailer parking legs, and release the trailer parking brake.

11. Before moving the tractor, check the brakes for proper functioning and for adequate air pressure; minimum operating air pressure is 60 pounds.

To uncouple a truck tractor from a semitrailer, proceed as follows:

1. Set the tractor hand brake.

2. Apply pressure to the trailer brakes by disconnecting the hose lines, as described above, step 5.

3. Disconnect the trailer electrical power lines and secure them to the tractor.

4. Place wheel chocks in front of and behind the trailer wheels and set the trailer parking brake.

5. Lower trailer parking legs; be sure the ground is firm enough to prevent the parking legs from sinking.

6. Place the fifth wheel hook lock handle in the release position; move the tractor foward slightly, leaving the trailer kingpin partly in the fifth wheel slot.

7. Recheck the trailer supports; if trailer is secure, move the tractor away from the trailer.

Safe Operation. In driving a tractor-trailer, watch for obstructions. Since a trailer body is often considerably higher than a truck body, you must allow for this height and watch out for viaducts, tree limbs, extended roofs OVER loading docks, and other obstructions. Also watch weight limitations on bridges. A tractor-trailer usually is longer than a truck; therefore, you must drive it carefully to avoid cutting in on other motorists.

Braking, Stopping, and Parking. With independently operated trailer brakes, apply the trailer brakes FIRST, gradually and smoothly, to avoid locking the wheels and skidding. As speed is reduced, apply the truck or tractor brakes to spread the braking load on all wheels. With synchronized brakes, both tractor and trailer brakes are operated by one foot pedal like the brakes on automobiles.

In making emergency stops, be sure the trailer brakes are applied either first or simultaneously with - never after - the tractor brakes. Attempting to stop without using the trailer brakes will cause the trailer load to push the tractor forward, and possibly push it into whatever you are trying to avoid.

In the event of any stop where you leave your cab, set your parking brake. This applies to all automotive equipment. If you have operated tractor-trailer units, you know that you can hold the unit on a grade by setting the trailer brake. Holding your rig on the grade by setting the trailer brake is all right AS LONG AS YOU ARE IN THE CAB, but DON'T set the trailer brake and LEAVE the cab. The engine on your rig may die and cause the air pressure to drop off. If this happens, your trailer brakes will release, and you will have a runaway rig.

Turning and Backing. In turning a tractor-trailer, remember that the outside turning circle of the complete unit is the same as that of the tractor, and that the trailer wheels cut inside the path of the tractor.

At first, it might seem that backing would be a difficult operation. Actually, the hinged-in-the-middle feature of tractor-trailer units makes them easier to handle in cramped quarters than conventional trucks.

If you wish to back your automobile or truck to the right, you would naturally turn the steering wheel to the right. To back your semitrailer to the right, you turn your steering wheel to the left. This action pushes the front of the semitrailer to the left and steers the semitrailer wheels to the right.

If you have to make a right-hand back into an alley (sometimes called a blind back), drive the unit past the alley entrance, keeping it far enough from the curb so that the tractor can head slightly to the right as you come to a stop.

Before you start to back, check behind the trailer from both sides of the cab to be sure of your distance, and that traffic is clear. Turn the steering wheel to the LEFT to push the semi-trailer around and back it to the right. As you continue to back slowly, keep the tractor wheels turned to the left and continue to check clearances from the right-hand door of the cab. As the trailer swings into the alley (with clearance on all sides), turn the steering wheel to the RIGHT and continue to back the semitrailer into the alley.

As the unit gets into line, straighten the front wheels and back down the alley, watching at all times to see that the semitrailer does not veer to either side. If the semitrailer angles to the left wall, adjust it to the right by turning your steering wheel to the left. If the semitrailer veers to the right, adjust it to the left by turning your steering wheel to the right.

A left-hand back is easier, because you can see the trailer from the driver's side of the cab. Of course, the direction you turn the steering wheel is just the opposite to a right-hand back.

Remember that to back the semitrailer to the right you turn the steering wheel to the left; and to back the semitrailer to the left, you turn the steering wheel to the right.

A skidding tractor-trailer unit is handled in a slightly different manner than a conventional vehicle. Turn your wheels immediately in the direction of the skid, accelerate slightly and (ONLY if the tractor is equipped with independent controlled brakes), apply the trailer brakes off and on gently so that the wheels will not lock. The trailer will then act as a drag and tend to pull both units back in line.

If the trailer starts to skid, handle it like a conventional vehicle, that is, do not apply brakes and turn in direction of skid.

BUSES

When operating buses to transport personnel, you will have responsibilities in addition to those concerning the operation of trucks and trailers.

Whether you operate a small shuttle bus on the base or a large passenger bus through a community from installation to installation, you are expected to observe a schedule of arrivals and departures, and to account for your runs.

Operation. The following rules for the operation of buses are supplementary to those applying to all motor vehicles:

1. Only operators with satisfactory records of safe driving will be assigned to drive buses.

2. Operators must be trained to stop, start, and operate buses smoothly and without jerks or sudden changes in acceleration.

3. Operators must not put vehicle in motion with the doors open,

4. Operators must not close the doors of a bus until passengers are completely clear of the bus when discharging, or fully inside and off the steps when entering the bus.

5. When making a turn or upon approaching a sharp curve, operators must reduce speed and use care to avoid injuring passengers.

6. The bus operator must give his attention to the road when driving and will not carry on unnecessary conversation with the passengers while the vehicle is in motion.

7. Operators of fare-charging buses will not make change while the bus is in motion.

Regulations. The driver of a school bus is required to exercise all precautions listed above in addition to the following special precautions:

1. Speed. No school bus will be driven at a speed greater than that authorized by the laws of the state in which the vehicle is being operated. When children are on the bus, the speed must be not more than 45 miles per hour.

2. Orderly Conduct. Passengers will be under the authority of and directly responsible to the operator of the bus, and the operator will be held responsible for the orderly conduct of the passengers.

3. Regular Stops . Pick up or discharge of any passenger except at regular stops designated is prohibited.

4. Railroad Crossings. Before crossing any railroad track or tracks, you must stop the bus within 50 feet but not less than 15 feet from the nearest rail of such railroad; while stopped, listen and look in both directions along the track for any approaching train; do not proceed until such precautions have been taken and until you have ascertained that the course is clear.

5. Crossing Street. Whenever a school bus stops to discharge passengers who must cross the street or highway in order to reach their destination, such passengers must cross in front of the bus, except when laws regulating local traffic prohibit this. In case of separated lanes with a median strip, the rule applies to both roadways. The bus must not be started until passengers desiring to cross have done so.

6. Escorting Children. The operator of a school bus must not permit pupils to cross a street or highway until they can do so safely; and he will, if necessary, secure the bus, dismount, and act as their escort.

The following precautions apply to operation of semitrailer buses:

1. Passengers

       a.   Standing in moving vehicles is prohibited except where handholds or straps are provided for each standee.

       b.   No passenger will be permitted to ride on running boards or with arms or legs extended outside the vehicle, or seated on fenders, top of cab, cab shields, or in door wells.

   c.   No passenger will be permitted to get on or off while the vehicle
         is in motion.

   2. Exit-Entrance

   a.   Exit-entrance on semitrailer buses without doors should be
         equipped with a heavy gage safety chain across the opening
         36 inches above floor level. Chains should be attached by a
         secure latching arrangement which will permit easy latching
         and unlatching.

   b.   The following signs must be posted at or near the inside of the
         exit and entrance of semitrailer buses not equipped with doors:

SITTING OR STANDING ON STEPS OR IN DOOR WELLS IS PROHIBITED

SAFETY CHAIN MUST BE LATCHED WHILE BUS IS IN MOTION

DUMP TRUCK OPERATION

During dumping operations, the truck should be on level ground or inclined uphill with front of truck facing downward. When the truck is in position, release the lower latches of the tailgate with the hand lever at the front left corner of the body. Now engage the power control with the dump body control lever, located in the cab. With the control lever at the farthest forward position, accelerate the engine moderately; do not race it. Hydraulic pressure will begin to hoist the dump body.

As the body rises, the load will slide backward under the open tailgate. If the load piles up and blocks the tailgate, place the truck in low gear and move it forward until there is more space to dump the remainder of the load. Do not change the position of the body control lever. If the load does not slide out easily, have someone dislodge it with a long hand shovel (taking care not to stand in the immediate dumping area). When dumping a load containing rocks or other large solids, the tailgate should be latched at the bottom, but unfastened at the top so that the tailgate can drop down and the load can drop. To spread a load over a large area, shift the truck into low gear and drive it slowly forward while dumping.

You can hold the body in any position by returning the control lever to position C. When dumping is completed, lower the body by returning the control lever to position A. Then close the tailgate latches.

TANK TRUCK OPERATION

Tank trucks are used to haul and dispense fuels or other types of liquids. A tank truck is equipped with a stainless steel, 1,200-gallon tank body, which is divided into two 600-gallon compartments. The fuel delivery system is equipped with an upright filter/separator and meter. Since there are only two tank compartments, the discharge valve control has two operating levers. There is a speed control linkage assembly which controls speed of the engine, power takeoff, and delivery pump.

The filter/separator is equipped with three filter elements, three go-no-go fuses, a pressure gage, and an automatic dump (drain) valve. The primary function of the filter element is to collect solid contaminants and separate water from the fuel.

The go-no-go fuses shut off the fuel flow if water or solid contaminants exceed a safe level; the shutoff of flow indicates that the filters are not operating properly. The malfunction must be located and corrected, and the fuses must be replaced before operation is continued.

The pressure gage reflects the condition of each of the filter elements and go-no-go fuses. When the pressure differential between the inlet pressure and the outlet pressure (gage handle in position 1) exceeds 20 psi, or when pressure differential between the inlet pressure and the internal pressure (gage handle in position 2) exceeds 15 psi, filter elements must be replaced. When pressure differential between outlet pressure and internal pressure (gage handle in position 3) exceeds 15 psi, replace the go-no-go fuses.

The automatic dump (drain) valve is float-operated. The float sinks in fuel but rises in water. When water is present in the valve housing, the float rises, the valve opens, and the water drains away through the valve drain tube. Open the automatic dump (drain) valve during fueling operations. Check pressure differential every day that equipment is in use; check it while the pump is operating, and record the readings.

When operating the fuel tank truck for discharging of fuels, follow instructions prescribed in the manufacturer's operating manual or the directions on the inside of the equipment compartment door. The general instructions which follow are typical.

Close the meter drain valve, delivery pump drain cock, and filter/separator drain valve. Open the automatic dump (drain) valve. Enter the driver's compartment and start the engine; depress the clutch, and put the transfer shift lever in neutral; place the transfer power takeoff shift lever in the engaged position; then place the transmission gearshift lever in fourth gear position, and release the clutch.

> CAUTION: Allowing the engine to run with transmission engaged and the transfer shift lever in neutral without the transfer power takeoff in the engaged position will cause bearing failure in the transfer case. Be sure to shift the transmission gearshift lever to neutral when not operating the power takeoff.

After the vehicle has been made ready, return to the fuel handling control compartment and set the remote hand throttle to allow the engine to operate at 700 rpm when the fuel dispensing pump is engaged. Move the discharge valve control operating lever of the tank compartment to be discharged to the open position; and be sure, before pumping operations begin, to attach the grounding wire to the vehicle being serviced. Open the pump delivery line hose and squeeze the nozzle operating lever and discharge the fuel. After discharging the fuel, close the pump delivery line gate valve, and move the discharge valve control operating lever to the closed position. Close the automatic dump valve drain tube valve and turn the hand throttle to the closed position. Return to the driver's compartment; depress

the clutch and place the transmission gearshift lever in neutral; then place the transfer power takeoff shifting lever to disengaged, and stop the engine.

When changing from one type of fuel to another, drain and flush the fuel compartment, pump filter/separator, service lines, manifold, meter, gage, and dispensing hoses and nozzles.

Remember, all pumping mechanisms are not controlled and operated in the same manner. You will find that each make or model will operate differently. If you are in doubt as to the proper pump operation and maintenance procedures, study the caution and instruction plates located near the pump and control mechanisms.

Drivers of fuel tank trucks must observe safe driving practices as listed below.

Drive defensively, and make allowances for other drivers.

Make turns only from proper lanes, and signal intent to other drivers. Never leave the proper lane except when necessary and then only when safe to do so.

Avoid excessive speeds at all times and especially on rough terrain, in gravel, and on curves. Be alert for passing or approaching traffic.

Drive downgrade in the same gear that would be used to drive upgrade.

Move completely off the road, if possible, when necessary to park. Set brakes, and chock wheels if stopping on a grade. Set flags during day and set flares or reflectors at night.

Stop at all railroad crossings, and be especially watchful in the case of multiple tracks.

Keep vehicle moving to prevent accumulations of vapor if a small leak develops in route. Arrange to discharge load at nearest point.

Ask for assistance if a large amount of fuel is escaping, such as might be the case if the vehicle is damaged. Immediately secure the engine, cordon the area, and obtain firefighting and security support.

Reduce refueling stops to a minimum under load. Stop the engine while refueling the prime mover.

Avoid driving past a fire or near the route until it is safe to do so.

Never smoke on or about tank vehicles used for hauling flammable liquids. Carry no matches on such vehicles.

Examine tires occasionally on long hauls for tire pressure and for damage that could cause an accident.

HAND SIGNALS

When you plan to turn, slow down, or stop, you must let the drivers approaching you and the drivers following you know well in advance what you intend to do.

The hand signals for these maneuvers are shown below. Instead of hand signals, mechanical directional signals may be used if your vehicle is so equipped. When operating vehicles in congested areas such as construction sites, docking areas, and pick-up and delivery areas, the hand signals depicted should be used.

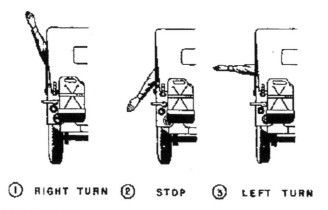

① RIGHT TURN ② STOP ③ LEFT TURN

HAZARDOUS CONDITIONS

Speed should always be reduced for night-time driving. Too many drivers try to drive just as fast at night as they do in the daytime.

Night driving is two to three times more dangerous than day driving. Fatigue and sharply reduced vision are the primary causes for increased danger. The steady hum of the motor and the darkness on the road ahead tend to lull us to sleep at the wheel. Wide-awake driving is necessary at all times and especially at night, since we can see objects only a limited distance ahead. After-dark driving requires different skills and extra care for safe driving.

Listed below are requirements and practices applicable to night driving which should be carefully observed:

1. When you meet a vehicle at night, you must lower your headlight beams when within 500 feet of the approaching vehicle.

2. Lower your headlight beams when following another vehicle within 200 feet.

3. Lower your headlight beams when you are driving on well-lighted streets.

4. Use your lower headlight beams when driving in a fog, and reduce your speed. Driving with your high beams in a fog is like shining your lights on a mirror — light is reflected back into your eyes and blinds you.

5. Avoid looking directly into the lights of vehicles that you are meeting. Instead, watch the right-hand edge of the road.

6. Keep your headlights properly adjusted so that the lower beams are not aimed upward into the approaching driver's eyes.

7. Keep your windshield clean.

8. Slow down when facing the glare from approaching headlights.

9. Be sure you can stop whenever necessary within the vision distance of your vehicle's headlights, and watch continually and carefully for pedestrians along the roadside.

10. Use your headlights during the period from one-half hour after sunset to one-half hour before sunrise, and whenever visibility is reduced.

When overtaking and passing other vehicles on the road, observe the common rules of passing. Use extreme caution whenever passing a vehicle as the view immediately beyond the other vehicle is blocked on that side. The greater the speed of the vehicle ahead, the more road space and time will be required to overtake and pass the vehicle,

Listed below are restrictions for overtaking and passing:

1. Do not pass to the right of another vehicle, except on multiple-lane divided highways (more than two lanes of traffic moving in one direction) and only then if such passing is permitted; use extreme caution in such instances.

2. Do not pass at an intersection or railroad crossing.

3. Do not pass on a hill or curve, except on multiple-lane, divided highways.

4. Do not pass a vehicle that is signaling to turn or to move into your lane of traffic, or one that has started to overtake and pass another vehicle.

5. Do not pass when the center line of the road is solid on your side.

6. Do not pass where the highway is divided by two solid lines.

7. Do not pass when the single center line is solid.

Rain, snow, ice, or fog affect visibility, stopping distance, maneuverability, and vehicle control. Follow these suggestions for driving under such conditions:

1. Adjust the speed of the vehicle to existing conditions.

2. For normal conditions, allow at least one car length between vehicles for every 10 mph that you are traveling. Increase the normal safe distance between vehicles to allow for wet conditions.

3. Use tire chains or snow tires on ice or snow; however, they are only an aid to increase traction and will not eliminate the necessity for added caution.

4. Slow down when approaching bridges, overpasses, and shady areas in the road; surfaces in such areas often freeze before regular roadway surfaces and remain frozen longer.

5. Keep the outside of the windshield and windows clear of snow, ice, and frost at all times, and use the vehicle defroster to improve visibility; use extreme caution when driving in fog.

6. Apply brakes with a light pumping action to prevent skidding and use engine compression to help control the vehicle.

7. Signal well in advance to warn others of an intended stop or turn.

Superhighways, designed for high speed driving, require drivers to be more skillful and alert to avoid accidents. When entering expressways, yield to all traffic. While traveling, allow necessary distance between vehicles for safe stopping; avoid highway hypnosis by making rest stops and opening vents or windows; and never exceed the posted speed. During emergencies, get the vehicle off the roadway; use flasher lights or flares behind the vehicle to warn other motorists; and look behind for oncoming or passing traffic before opening vehicle doors. When leaving expressways, get in the proper lane well before the turn-off, and use turn signals to warn other drivers.

When driving through water, reduce speed to prevent brake drums, engine, and ignition from getting wet. Test the brakes for effectiveness immediately after leaving the water. If water has entered the brake drums and wet the linings, drive at a very slow speed while gently applying sufficient pressure on the brake pedal to cause a slight drag, thereby squeezing the brake linings against the drums and forcing the water out of the linings.

Snow and Ice. Snow and ice severely limit the traction of any vehicle. To increase traction, put chains on all driving wheels. When moving over fresh snow, maintain a slow, steady speed. Rapid acceleration is likely to cause skidding, or cause the wheels to dig in. If your vehicle becomes stuck in a hole in the snow, rocking it back and forth by shifting from forward to reverse may enable you to start again. Brakes, when used, should be applied lightly and released quickly if skidding begins. If you are driving hauling equipment that includes a trailer, apply only the trailer brakes, or at least apply them first.

Hard packed snow or ice is even more dangerous to drive on than newly fallen snow. Snow tires are not much help on ice, as they add little or no traction and give you a false feeling of security. Deflating the tires a bit will assist in preventing skidding.

Mud, Sand, and Swamps. When approaching a stretch of sticky soil or of muddy or swampy ground, put chains on the rear wheels to save yourself a lot of distress. If chains are not available, and the going looks rough, go into the necessary low gear. Engage the front-wheel drive, if the vehicle has one. Size up the road ahead so that once you start you can keep going. As far as possible, avoid ruts, holes, and edges that may cause side slips and swaying loads. Speed should be maintained, but do not spin the wheels. If the wheels start to lose traction, decrease speed but stay in the same gear. If the vehicle should become hopelessly bogged down, do not spin the wheels and burn up the tires, and do not overtax the equipment. Instead disengage the clutch at once, and get out and look the situation over. How to get out of bad situations depends on circumstances.

You may be able to back out and select a better way through. If you have wheel mats, use them. You may be able to jack up one wheel and place brush, boards, rocks, or similar material under it, enabling you to pull out. You may be able to dig your way out by digging a ditch in the direction that the wheels are expected to move. When the wheels are in deep ruts, ditches dug at an angle to the ruts may be necessary to assist the wheels back to a straddle position over the rut.

Of course, if a suitable tow truck is available, use it to get out of trouble. If your piece of equipment is equipped with a winch, use it to pull yourself out.

If the truck has dual wheels, use two tow ropes and six strong stakes. Drive two stakes into the ground the same distance apart as the wheels. Drive these stakes in front of the truck, if the best route out is forward, and behind if the best route out is backward. Use the other four stakes as anchors. The loop ends of the tow ropes are secured to the wheels by passing them between the duals, out through the spokes, and over the hub. The ropes are then attached to the anchor stakes. When this is done, the vehicle can move out on its own power by allowing the tow ropes to wind up between the dual wheels.

If stuck in sand, chicken wire on heavy burlap or canvas tarpaulins staked to the surface will aid greatly in supporting the load of the truck - and usually will get you out. In some cases, sand is somewhat encrusted below the surface and the vehicle will continue to creep forward even though the wheels spin. As long as the vehicle continues to move, the wheels may be kept spinning slowly, allowing your vehicle to dig its way out. Do not allow the vehicle to develop a differential jump; should this occur, STOP VEHICLE and try another solution. You may have to let some of the air out of your tires to pull through a stretch of sand but, as a general rule, it is bad practice to run on underinflated tires. In going through sand, as in going through other tough spots, it is essential to maintain momentum and keep going. Changing of gears must be avoided by selecting the proper gear before entering the sand.

Fording. Before you start through water, whether fording or crossing a stretch of flooded highway, be sure that the water is not so deep that it will drown out your motor. Also make sure that the surface under the water will support your vehicle. As a rule, nothing is gained by attempting to use momentum in crossing streams or other water. Cross slowly in a low gear. If there is any danger of water surging or splashing into the fan, disconnect it before crossing. After crossing the stream, apply the brakes intermittently until dry, enough to hold. At the first opportunity, wheels, crank-case, universal joint, differential, transmission, and other parts submerged should be checked to determine that no water has entered.

SECURING

When returning to the equipment pool area at the end of the day's run, top off fuel tanks, check oil and coolant levels, and position vehicle in a safe manner. Let engine idle, check instrument readings, secure footbrake or handbrake, place transmission in neutral, secure engine by turning off ignition switch, complete daily trip ticket, roll up windows, secure doors, block vehicle if required, drain air tanks (if so equipped), and turn in required reports to the dispatcher,

IV. OPERATOR'S MAINTENANCE

Every equipment operator is required to perform certain daily maintenance services on his vehicle as a matter of routine. The faithful performance of these services does much to prolong the life of the vehicle, to avoid major repairs and overhaul, and to assure the equipment operator that his vehicle will perform consistently and dependably. *Operator's maintenance* is the term that describes the required inspection, service, lubrication, and adjustments performed by an operator to keep power tools and equipment in a safe operable condition, in order to prevent personnel injuries, mechanical malfunctions, and curtailment of production or progress.

FAN BELTS

Worn or loose fan belts are often the cause of engine overheating, especially when the engine is operating in low or second gear. Excessive looseness or tightness can be determined by applying the manufacturer's specified pressure to the belt at a point midway between the fan and the generator pulleys and determining that the deflection is within the range specified for the vehicle.

If it.is necessary to adjust the fan belt, first look at the type of device used to provide the fan takeup and follow the manufacturer's adjusting procedures.

IGNITION AND ELECTRICAL SYSTEMS

Ignition troubles are often a major cause of improper engine performance. When an ignition tuneup is required, it includes checking the battery, cleaning and inspecting all wires and terminals, cleaning or replacing and adjusting spark plugs, checking ignition timing, and adjusting breaker points. These are important jobs in an ignition tuneup, but you are only required to check the battery and clean and inspect all wires and terminals. An experienced mechanic using proper equipment will adjust and check timing and ignition breaker points, and clean or replace and adjust spark plugs to the manufacturer's specifications.

BATTERY AND BATTERY CONNECTIONS

The storage battery supplies power for all electrical accessories. The condition of the battery is the first concern in accessory maintenance. Check the battery periodically for water, and see that the battery terminals are tight and free from corrosion. If the battery fails to supply sufficient power to turn the starter or to operate other electrical units on a vehicle, report this malfunction to the maintenance section for corrective action.

Most electrical troubles can be traced to poor ground connections, loose wire connections, and worn or frayed wires that cause short circuits, rather than to a defective battery.

Tightening a loose wire connection is a simple operation; a worn, frayed, or broken wire should be taped to make temporary repairs ONLY. The vehicle should be taken to the shop where a mechanic will replace the wire with a new one.

COOLING SYSTEM

You will need to drain the coolant from the cooling system occasionally to remove sediment and rust scales and for periodic radiator flushing. Be sure all the coolant is removed. The manufacturer's maintenance manuals will show you the locations of drain cocks and plugs, which are usually found in the lowest points of the systems.

When refilling a cooling system that has been drained, allow water to pass through the engine and out the drain openings before closing them. When the water is clear and flows freely from the openings, close them securely and fill the cooling system slowly. Never add water faster than it can circulate through the various branches of the system, since water overflowing from the cap may give a false indication of a full system. Do not add water to the cooling system of an overheated engine; allow the engine to cool first. If you must add water before you are sure the engine is cool, run the engine and add water very slowly. Cold water in an overheated engine may crank a cylinder block or cause other serious damage to engine parts.

WHEELS AND TIRES

You should become familiar with the recommendations of tire manufacturers on the proper use and care of tires on vehicles. Probably one of the most common mistakes is incorrect tire pressure. To keep vehicles operating continuously and efficiently, you must follow the procedures recommended by the manufacturer for inspecting and inflating tires. To get the maximum life from a tire, you must maintain proper tire pressure to match the load the vehicle will carry at its actual operating speed. You must make periodic pressure checks on cold tires (before running equipment), and make visual inspection of tires for tread cuts, sidewall snags, and wear. Check wheel rims for splits, metal fatigue, and out-of-round condition.

When tires are to be removed, take the equipment to the tire shop, where special tools and personnel are available to replace or repair the tires. You will be required to help the tire repair personnel to disassemble and repair the tire. Detailed procedures on this will be given later in the chapter.

BRAKE SYSTEMS

When inspecting hydraulic brakes, ensure that the proper level of hydraulic fluid is maintained in the master cylinder reservoir, and check the system for leaks and worn parts. Be sure to add the kind of hydraulic fluid recommended by the manufacturer, because some brake systems are made with natural rubber seals and others with synthetic seals. Unless the recommended fluid is used, the seals will deteriorate quickly and the hydraulic brakes will not operate.

Dust and dirt that accumulates around the filler plug opening can also affect brake operation. A small particle of dust or dirt that may find its way into the operating mechanism can close a vent or prevent a valve from seating properly. See that all dust and dirt are removed before you uncover the master cylinder and add fluid. Add enough fluid so that the level reaches just below the filler plug opening. After filling the reservoir, see that the vent at the top of the reservoir is open and the filler plug is tight.

Leaks and loose joints in the brake system not only allow fluid to escape but also permit air to enter. Air in the hydraulic system can be felt by the soft, springy action of the brake pedal, and must be removed by bleeding to obtain a solid pedal. When bleeding becomes necessary, take the vehicle to the maintenance shop, where special tools and personnel are available to correct the situation.

When inspecting and servicing airbrake systems, the most common problem you will find is leaking air lines. The air line hoses and couplings should be checked for leaks and wear, particularly those connecting a truck and trailer. Replace worn hoses and tighten hose connections and couplings. The cutout cocks provided at the tractor hose connections are often responsible for air loss. These tapered valves should be checked often and kept tightly closed. When no trailer is being towed, they often jar open. Be sure these valves are closed tightly, but are free to open when trailer brakes are required. A little penetrating oil will free a binding cutout cock.

The drain cock at each air reservoir should work freely. Reservoirs should be drained daily to remove water that accumulates from condensation.

BODY AND FRAME

The mobility of trailers results in frequent shipment of vehicles, with consequent likelihood of damage to the body and frame during shipment. Of course, accidents are another cause of body and frame damage.

During the operator's maintenance, he will inspect the body and frame of the vehicle. He will look for damaged portions of the body and report the damage so that repairs can be made by the body shop personnel. These body repairs include straightening body panels, replacing body parts, and repainting.

If damage to the frame is detected by your inspection, this will also be reported and the body shop personnel allowed to repair the damage, if they are equipped to do so. If they do not have the equipment, the vehicle must be sent to a larger repair facility equipped with frame straightening machines.

LUBRICATING OIL SYSTEM

Check the oil level and, if necessary, add additional oil for a full gage or dipstick reading. Do not overfill.

If the oil feels gritty to the fingers or has no body, it has lost its effective lubricating qualities and must be changed.

Oil changes should also be made in accordance with the manufacturers' lubrication and maintenance schedules. On most of your equipment, the grade and quantity of the oil to be used will be found on the lubricating charts.

Drain the oil only after the engine has run and is warmed up. This warmup period will thin the oil and stir up the sludge and foreign matter in the oil pan. After replacing with new oil, recheck the oil level to be certain that the oil column reaches the full mark on the dipstick. Then run the engine for a few minutes to ensure no leaks exist, particularly around the oil filter and the oil drain plug. Get into the habit of looking at the ground or pavement over which the vehicle has been parked, for any oil spots that may indicate leakage.

Changing oil filter elements periodically will be part of your job. Usually the filter elements are changed at the same time the oil is changed in the crankcase. On new engines, it may be changed (1) after the first 500 miles; (2) according to the manufacturer's instructions; or (3) according to shop policy. The filter element should be replaced with the type recommended by the manufacturer. Be sure to remove the old gasket and see that the new gasket under the cover or in the crankcase is properly fitted, and that there are no oil leaks. Always check these points immediately after starting the engine.

FUEL SYSTEM

The fuel system consists of the fuel tank, fuel pump, carburetor, intake manifold, and fuel lines or tubes connecting the tank, pump, and carburetor.

Fuel tanks give little or no trouble, and as a rule require no servicing other than an occasional draining and cleaning. If, during inspection, you should find the fuel tank either punctured or leaking, report the trouble, leaving the repairs or replacement to the repair shop where there are proper servicing facilities. All fuel leaks will be considered cause for immediate shutdown.

If the presence of gasoline in the crankcase is observed, it is a good indication of a diaphragm leaking within the fuel pump. Usually, the mechanics will replace the pump or repair it using a repair kit for this purpose.

Inspect the fuel lines and connections, observing that the lines are placed away from the exhaust pipes, mufflers, and manifolds so that excessive heat will not cause vaporlock. Make sure fuel lines are attached to the frame, engine, and other units so that the effects of the vibration will be minimized. Fuel lines should be free of contact with sharp edges which might cause wear. In places of excessive movement, as between the vehicle frame and rubber-mounted engine, short lengths of gasoline-resistant flexible tubing are used. Occasionally, road vibration may loosen and break lines, and they can become pinched or flattened by flying rocks. Such damage could interfere with the flow of fuel.

A certain amount of scale forms within the fuel lines and sometimes causes a stoppage.

When, in the course of your daily maintenance services of the fuel system, you observe operational troubles with the carburetor, report the troubles, leaving the adjustments, repairs, or replacement of the carburetor with the maintenance personnel equipped to handle these troubles.

V. LUBRICATION

As you may recall, lubricants act as cooling agents, sealing agents, cleaning agents, and reduce friction and wear. This section discusses the procedures of lubrication.

Periodic lubrication prolongs the usefulness of a vehicle. Proper lubrication is more than merely placing a grease gun on a fitting and pulling the trigger. It means selecting the correct lubricants and applying them in a sufficient amount and in the proper places. The experienced equipment operator uses neither too much nor too little lubricant.

Lubrication, then, is a thorough job of oiling and greasing. The lube rack will likely carry several approved standard lubricants. This standardization of lubricants eliminates the variation and confusion in manufacturer's brand names and quality designations, and makes readily available a few standard lubricants.

Familiarize yourself with the lubrication chart of the vehicle with which you are working. These charts show what to lubricate, and where.

Of course, you must learn to use grease guns properly, as well as other dispensers of oils and grease.

Remember that grease on the outside of a fitting does not lubricate, and oil or grease in puddles or gobs around the grease rack can cause serious injury. So look for and remove spilled oil or grease that drops from chassis parts. Better yet, while lubricating a piece of equipment, remove all excessive grease from the fittings and wipe up lubricants that fall to the floor.

DISPENSING LUBRICANTS

Grease guns and dispensers operate either by hand or are air operated. You have probably used the hand-operated <u>muzzle-loader</u> type of grease gun. This grease gun can be taken apart to load it with grease. It is generally used in places hard to reach with a pressure gun, or in lubricating water pumps and other accessories requiring a special lubricant. Lubricants used for most chassis parts, however, are forced through the fittings by guns operated by air pressure.

Crankcase oil is generally dispensed with measured containers or with a hand- or air-operated pumping system. Hand- or air-operated systems normally have meters that register the amount of oil dispensed, Gear box lubricants are generally dispensed by some type of hand-or air-operated pumping system. Be sure you use the right lubricant dispensers. To prevent mistakes, each dispenser is marked to show the grade and type of lubricant it contains.

Before using the lubrication gun, all fittings which are to be lubricated MUST be properly cleaned to avoid forcing dirt into the bearing.

The proper technique for using the lubrication gun is essential. Improper use of the gun can damage the hydraulic coupler jaws and can also damage the fitting. Damaged coupler jaws will prevent proper sealing with fittings. To prevent damage, press the coupler straight onto the <u>clean</u> fitting.

CAUTION: Care must be exercised when using a high pressure lube gun on certain lube points. Excessive pressure can damage or *blow off* the grease seals and/or dust caps. To prevent this damage, apply grease by one or two quick pulls on the trigger; this prevents excess pressure building up in the seals.

After a vehicle is lubricated, clean and fill the grease guns. Then check them to see if they are working properly. Next see that they and other lubricating equipment are stowed in their proper places. Take an inventory of your tools to be sure they are not carried away on the vehicle frame or running board.

CHASSIS LUBRICATION

Most chassis lubrication fittings are located on the front suspension and steering mechanisms. The importance of proper chassis lubrication cannot be overstressed. This lubrication should always be performed in accordance with the manufacturer's lubrication charts.

Frozen fittings will not readily accept lubricants because the friction surface containing the fitting has dry and dirty working surfaces. Some relative motion in the connection is needed to permit

the lubricant to enter the frozen fitting. Vertical rocking of the vehicle is the usual method of providing this relative motion in the coupling. In some extreme cases, it may be necessary to disassemble the unit being greased in order to properly lubricate it. NEVER pass up a frozen fitting.

BODY LUBRICATION

To lubricate the hood, apply a few drops of oil on the fastener-and-release mechanism, coat the fastener pins and hooks with a light application of dry stick lubricant, and close the hood.

Car doors and trunk lids are lubricated by applying a drop or two of oil to the door latch and trunk lid mechanisms. Also apply a few drops of oil to the hinges and swing the door back and forth or raise and lower the lid to spread the lubricant over the contacting surfaces; wipe off any excess lubricant.

The door striker assembly is lubricated by applying a light coating of dry stick lubricant to all sliding surfaces and a few drops of oil to all bearing surfaces. Apply a drop or two of oil around the edge of the cylinder face and to the outer surface of pushbutton latches and press the pushbuttons several times to distribute the lubricant. Wipe off any excess oil and lubricants.

Never use oil to lubricate locks since it collects dust and lint. Inject graphite directly into the keyhole and work the lock several times to distribute the graphite in the tumbler mechanism.

A dry stick lubricant is best used for sliding weather-stripping surfaces of ashtrays, hinged visors, glove compartments, and other hinged units within the vehicle. Hinged surfaces outside of the vehicle may be lubricated lightly with oil. Always remember that the few minutes it requires to oil these various items will, in most cases, eliminate their failure.

Generator Service. Periodic lubrication service is required by most generators. A few generators have sealed bearings which require no lubrication. The generator should be lubricated only at those intervals specified by the manufacturer's lubrication chart.

Distributor Service. The distributor requires service lubrication at three points - the shaft bearing, the centrifugal spark advance mechanism, and the cam. The shaft bearing is lubricated through either an oil cup, grease fitting, or grease cup. Some distributors are equipped with a removable access plug to the shaft bearing reservoir.

The automatic spark centrifugal advance mechanism may be lubricated through a small, round felt wick located at the top of the distributor shaft. Apply two or three drops of motor oil to the

felt wick. With your fingertip, apply a light film of high temperature type grease to the cam. CAUTION: Excess lubricant on the cam may be thrown over to the points and cause ignition failure.

Steering Gear Service. The fluid level in the gear housing should be checked at every chassis lubrication. You should clean around the fill plug on top of the steering gear housing before removing the fill plug. Do not disturb the adjusting screw locknut adjacent to the fill plug. Check the lubricant level and add lubricant, if necessary, to bring the lubricant level to the bottom of the fill plug hole. You then replace the fill plug.

Three points require lubrication in power steering systems. The gear housing is serviced as above on the linkage type of power steering. As you may recall, the linkage type of power steering system has the power cylinder and control valve connected to the steering linkage and a steering gear of conventional design. Additional lubrication fittings under the car may be found on the power cylinder or the power cylinder attachment points in the linkage type. The fluid reservoir is serviced at each chassis lubrication by cleaning the area, removing the dipstick or reservoir cover, checking the oil level, and replacing the dipstick or cover after adding oil if necessary. Power systems can become inoperative due to dirt in the system, so use care to prevent dirt from entering the reservoir during service operations.

Brake Service. The fluid level in the hydraulic brake master cylinder should be checked at every chassis lubrication. The fluid level must be visually checked at the reservoir. Pumping the brake pedal does not constitute a complete check. Service the master cylinder by cleaning the area around the fill plug, removing the fill plug, checking the fluid level and refilling the master cylinder reservoir to within half an inch below the fill hole, and replacing the gasket and fill plug. Always use the hydraulic fluid recommended by the manufacturer's lubrication chart. The use of inferior brake fluid or one which contains mineral oil will result in deterioration of the rubber seal, making it necessary to completely overhaul the brake system and flush all brake lines.

FAN BELT ADJUSTMENTS

There are many types of fan belts and many procedures used for adjusting them. It is beyond the scope of this manual to present information on all types of fan belts. Therefore, the following information presented should familiarize you with fan belt adjustments in general.

Check the fan belt (sometimes called a drive belt) tension by applying the manufacturer's specified pressure to the belt at a point midway between the fan and the generator pulley. Belt deflection at this point should be as specified. If belt deflection is found to be more or less than specified, adjust tension as follows:

1. Loosen generator-to-adjusting-arm capscrew.

2. Insert end of pry bar between crankcase and generator so that the lower end of the bar will bear against crankcase.

3. Pull upper end of pry bar away from engine with a pull of approximately 50 pounds, and keep handle in this position; then tighten the generator-to-adjustment-arm capscrew. This procedure will place belts under proper tension and allow for specified belt deflection.

HANDBRAKE ADJUSTMENT

In most automotive vehicles, the handbrake has its own hookup. Either external-contracting brake bands are located on the drive shaft or some type of mechanical linkage operates the rear wheel brakes.

Handbrake controls consist of a handbrake lever connected by linkage to the brake shoe lever at the rear of the transfer case. The handbrake is properly adjusted when it will hold the vehicle on an incline with the handbrake lever moved one-third of the way in reverse, or if application of the brake at a speed of 10 mph stops the vehicle within a reasonable distance.

To increase braking action of the handbrake, turn the knurled end of the handbrake lever clockwise. To decrease braking action (to prevent dragging of the brake shoes), turn the knurled end counterclockwise. If braking action cannot be increased sufficiently by turning the knurled end clockwise, turn the knurled end counterclockwise, adjust linkage tension at the brake shoe lever, and then turn the knurled end clockwise until the correct brake adjustment is obtained. To adjust linkage at brake shoe lever, hold adjusting nut on transfer end of linkage, loosen locknut, turn adjusting nut clockwise on linkage, and tighten locknut.

VI. TIRES

Pneumatic tires and inner tubes are designed to provide traction and cushion the shocks of the road or terrain. Traction is provided by the natural friction of the rubber upon contact with the road or terrain, aided by the tread design of the tire. Cushioning is provided largely by the air within the tube, or the tire itself if of tubeless design. Both tires and tube are flexible enough to *give* when a bump or chuck hole is struck, and they are able to resume their former shape immediately.

CHANGING A TIRE

A word of CAUTION before you lift a vehicle with a jack to change a tire: If you are to jack either of the rear wheels, place a block or stone in front of both front wheels to keep the vehicle from rolling forward and off the jackj if you jack either of the front wheels, place the block or stone behind both rear wheels.

To remove the wheel, remove the hubcap, which snaps into spring clips. Then remove the five or six hub bolts or nuts that fasten the wheel to the wheel hub. Wheels on the right side are fastened with right-hand thread bolts or nuts, and those on the left side with left-hand thread bolts or nuts to eliminate the tendency to loosen with wheel rotation. In raising the wheel from the ground, be careful not to push the vehicle off the jack. The spare wheel and tire should be placed on the vehicle immediately.

Removing dual disk wheels to change tires on heavy vehicles is not too difficult. Generally, both disks are fastened together by two nuts on each hub bolt - one nut for each wheel. Either single or dual wheels can be securely mounted on the same hub with this arrangement. Outer nuts must be loosened first, freeing the outer wheel disk from the hub. Loosening the outer nuts, which thread over the inner nuts, unfastens the outer wheel disk. In removing dual disk wheels, you will find left-hand threads on both inner and outer nuts on the left wheels and right-hand threads on those of the right wheels. Reverse the procedure to mount and tighten the wheels.

On trucks having spoke wheels, the tire and tube are removed with the rim. After removing the clamps which secure the rim on the spoke spider, the rim with the tire and tube can be lifted off. If the spoke wheel has two rims and tires, the second rim and tire can be lifted off after the spacer separating the rims is removed. In replacing the tires, the inner rim should be placed so that the valve stem can be reached easily for periodic inflation.

A tire demounter should be used to remove a tire from the rim.

In mounting a tubed tire, inflate the tube until it is almost round. Put the inside bead of the tire on the rim and insert the tube into the tire with the valve at the red (balance) mark on the tire. Guide the valve stem through the valve hole. Be sure the valve stem is pointed in the right direction if you are mounting the tire for use on dual wheels. And if it is a rubber stem, see that the stem enters the hole without bending.

The first bead will slide in rather easily, but the second bead may offer a little trouble. Use the tire irons, and work both ways from the stem to slide both tire beads in the rim walls. DO NOT PINCH THE TUBE. Use a rubber mallet (NOT a hammer) to strike the center of the tread around the tire to help seat the second bead and the tube properly. On other than drop center rims, see that the lock rings are securely fastened.

Inflate the tire slowly after mounting it on the rim. See that the tire beads fit snugly against the rim flanges, and that lock rings are turned face down and remain in the locked position. Serious accidents can result from failure to observe these precautions. Too much pressure applied at once can cause a lock ring to fly off the rim or the tire itself to be blown off and seriously injure personnel. Inflate tires inside a steel tire cage. This will confine the tire enough to keep it from striking you in case either it or the ring bursts its fittings.

TUBELESS TIRES

Most of the lighter and heavier vehicles now are equipped with tubeless tires. Instead of being sealed in an inner tube, the air in these tires is sealed in a space between the outer casing and the rim. Both this space and the point of contact of the tire against the rim must be airtight. The rim, on which the valve for inflating the tire is mounted, becomes a part of the air retaining chamber. When using tire irons, exercise care not to tear or otherwise injure the sealing ribs or beads on the tire being repaired.

Before replacing a tubeless tire, examine the rim carefully for dents, roughness, and rust, any of which may impair or break the air seal. Straighten out any dents with a hammer, and use steel wool to clean the bead seat area of any rust or grit. If the rim is badly bent or out of round, a new wheel should be installed on the vehicle.

Removing and remounting a tubeless tire are similar to the operations for tubed tires. If the tire seal is broken or defective, it will be necessary to use a tube inside the tire. Otherwise, the tire will lose air, and you will have to inflate it frequently. Some tubeless passenger car tires must be removed from the rear of the rim to prevent stretching the bead wires too far and causing them to break. If in doubt about any other details of changing tubeless tires, follow the tire manufacturer's instructions, or consult with your supervising petty officer.

ROTATING TIRES

Rotating tires is recommended by the manufacturer. If several tires show more wear than others, or if the mileage is approaching another mile interval, you will rotate all the vehicle's tires in the following manner:

1. On automobiles having a spare tire, the left front tire should be moved to the left rear, the right front to the spare, the two rears to the opposite front wheels, and the spare to the right rear.

2. On automobiles having no spare, move the front tires to the rear on the same side, and move the rear to the opposite front wheels.

3. On vehicles having six tires (dual tires on rear), new tires should normally be mounted on the front wheels for one-third of their life, then moved to the outside rear wheels for another third, and finally shifted to the rear inside wheels. A few service conditions which demand maximum traction on rear wheels may require that new tires, or tires with relatively good treads, be mounted on the rear wheels.

CAUSES OF TIRE WEAR

Pneumatic tires have been installed on many items of equipment to increase mobility and efficiency. However, unless tires are properly cared for, much of this efficiency and mobility is lost to the user.

Probably the greatest factor in prolonging the life of pneumatic tires is proper inflation. Correct tire pressure cannot be checked by kicking the tire. It requires the use of a pressure gage. Tire pressure checks should be made prior to the vehicle being moved. This can be accomplished during the *Before Operation Services.* (Don't forget to check the spare tire.) If the pressure is neglected, the results can be costly. Tire pressure should be stenciled on the dash or fenders.

Abnormal wear from improper tire inflation can be divided into four categories. These are: overinflation, overinflation-impact injury, underinflation, and underinflation injury. Let's look at each of these in detail, and learn how to get maximum life from our tires.

Overinflation stretches the tire and permits only the center section of the tread to come in contact with the road. Since the wear is concentrated on the central part of the tread, the indication of overinflation is wear in the center of the tread. An overinflated tire has no give and is constantly subjected to hard jolts, causing the drive wheels to bounce and spin, literally abrashing the rubber. There is also less tire to road surface contact with an overinflated tire, and this causes a safety hazard in both braking and sliding.

An overinflated tire is more susceptible to impact injury because the cords are stretched tight. In this condition, the tire will not give or flex and distribute the shock over a great area of the ply cords.

The external indication of an underinflated tire is more wear on the edges than in the center of the tread. Underinflation causes excessive movement and scuffing between the tire and the road, which in turn results in faster tread wear. There may be occasions when chains are not available and tire pressures must be lowered to get better traction in sand, ice, mud, and snow. When this occurs, prescribed pressures for these conditions should be maintained to prevent tire damage.

The excessive flexing and movement of the ply cords cause a tire to get hot resulting in separation of cords and rubber. When the cords are separated from the body, the tire is permanently damaged and must be replaced. This replacement is a direct result of operator neglect and not fair wear and tear. While the tire must be removed from the wheel to properly identify this condition, in many instances radial cracks will appear on the outer wall of the tire which will serve as a warning that the tire has been operated underinflated.

All uneven tire wear is not caused by improper inflation. Wear of this type can be caused by wheels out of line or improperly balanced, excessive toe-in or toe-out, or improper camber. Uneven tire wear can also be caused by operating a vehicle with the front wheel drive engaged on dry hard surfaced roads. When uneven tire wear occurs, the mechanical defects must be corrected immediately and the tires rotated.

The proper selection and mounting of tires for dual assemblies is extremely important. Mismatched tires cause uneven distribution of the load which defeats the purpose of the duals. In this case, the larger tire carries the greater load, subjecting it to excessive wear and early failure. Also, the smaller tire wears more rapidly than normal. It scuffs along without sufficient road traction causing excessive wear. Since you are not always able to match sizes of tires exactly, except with new tires, certain tolerances are allowed. The larger of the two duals should always be mounted on the outside so that they will conform to the *crown* of the road and shoulder the load more evenly.

Directional bar tread is commonly used on road graders and other earthmoving equipment. The bars and open center pattern are designed to permit each bar to dig in deep, take a firm hold, and give maximum traction in soft, muddy, or slippery surfaces. Since this is a directional tread tire, it must be mounted on live axles so the point of the *V* comes in contact with the ground first. When the directional tire is mounted in this manner, it is *self-cleaning*. It forces the dirt and mud out to the side. When the directional tread tire is mounted on a towed vehicle or on a dead axle, it is mounted so that the open part of the 7 meets the ground first.

An insignificant little thing, but absolutely necessary, is the valve cap. This cover keeps dirt, water, and grit out of the valve and provides the final seal against air escaping from the tube. For speed and convenience in inflating, valve stems should be readily accessible. They should be positioned to prevent rubbing against the brake drum and to extend through the wheel hand holes. Ends of valves on front wheels and inside duals point away from the vehicle. Valves on outside duals point toward the vehicle. On dual wheels, valves are placed 180° apart for convenience in checking pressure and inflating.

Rims and rim flanges should be checked regularly to be sure that they are in good condition and fit properly. Since the flange comes in direct contact with the bead which supports the tire, flanges that are bent, broken, chipped, or of the wrong size put a terrific strain on the bead and lead to early tire failure.

Most of the larger wheels and rims used on equipment are the lockring type. The use of the lockring makes tire changing much easier and faster than on the one piece rim of the same size. The principle of the lockring is simple, requiring only that the lockring be firmly seated in the gutter of the rim base. When this is done, the tire and wheel will perform equally as well as the one piece riri. While there is a high safety factor built into the tire and rim assembly, danger results from carelessness or negligence in assembly. Before starting the inflate, make sure that all rim parts are correctly assembled and interlocking. It is recommended that inflation cages, safety chains, or some other safety device be used during inflation. Rims and lockrings should be inspected periodically for damage. A damaged rim or lockring should be replaced immediately as this will create a safety hazard and may ruin a tire. A displaced lockring may spring loose and can result in serious injury or death to personnel who may be in the vicinity.

When should we replace worn tires? This is a very important question because tires worn beyond the prescribed limit cannot be recapped. If you cannot grip the tread with your thumb and index finger, ask your supervisor for technical assistance to determine if replacement is required. When the tread design is worn off in the center so that the tire is smooth across the center, the tire should be replaced.

Make careful checks for damage due to vehicle obstructions. Spring clips, fender bolts, exhaust pipes, etc. may be set in a satisfactory location when the vehicle is at a standstill. But under unusual operating conditions, the body movement may cause these units to contact the tire and cause severe abrasion. The tires of low bed trailers and trailer-mounted air compressors are highly susceptible to this type damage.

Rocks or dry caked mud should be removed from between dual assemblies as soon as possible. Extensive tire damage can also be caused by snow and ice packed between duals or under fenders and cross braces in winter operation. Any such materials coming in contact with tires while they are in operation can cause severe cuts or abrasions.

———

Made in the USA
San Bernardino, CA
02 December 2019